The Racing BIKE BOOK

Steve Thomas

Ben Searle

Dave Smith

Updated by

Steve Thomas

Hilary Stone

Joe Beer

Haynes

THE BOOK

Written by: Steve Thomas, Ben Searle, Dave Smith
Updated by: Steve Thomas, Hilary Stone and Joe Beer
Editor: Caroline Arthur
Art director: Graham Webb
Location photography: Steve Behr
Studio photography: Nick Pope
Illustrations: Ron Mercer
Project manager: Louise McIntyre

Steve Thomas, Ben Searle and Dave Smith have asserted their rights to be identified as the authors of this work.

First published 1997
© Haynes Publishing 1997
2nd Edition published 2000
3rd Edition published 2007

All rights reserved. No part of this publication may be reproduced, stored in a retrieval system or transmitted, in any form or by any means, electronic, mechanical, photocopying, recording or otherwise, without prior permission in writing from the publisher.

Published by: Haynes Publishing
Sparkford, Nr Yeovil, Somerset BA22 7JJ
Tel: 01963 442030 Fax: 01963 440001
Int. tel: +44 1963 442030 Fax: +44 1963 440001
E-mail: sales@haynes.co.uk
Web site: www.haynes.co.uk

British Library Cataloguing-in-Publication Data:
A catalogue record for this book is available from the British Library.

ISBN 978 1 84425 341 8

Printed in England by
J. H. Haynes & Co Ltd, Sparkford.

While every effort is taken to ensure the accuracy of the information given in this book, no liability can be accepted by the authors or the publisher for any loss, damage or injury caused by errors in, or omissions from, the information given.

CONTENTS

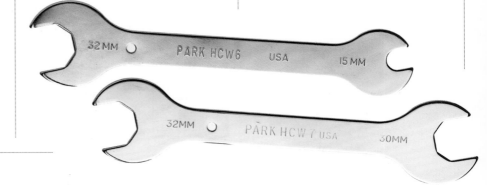

Foreword

Cycling is a great sport, a fabulous pastime and, for me, a great way of life. I started cycling longer ago than I care to remember, but even after nearly two decades of riding as a professional, winning many of the greatest honours within the sport and suffering the many painful hardships those achievements demand, I still get the same buzz as I always have done from going out and riding with the local club at the weekend, talking to the guys, sprinting for the road signs. To me, that's the most important thing of all.

My career as a professional was very much a learning process. Starting out from Ireland, a country without any real bike-racing tradition, I set off for Europe, the hotbed of cycling, to carry out my apprenticeship. There I learned how to suffer more, how to train better and how to think more clearly, and all this hard-won knowledge has helped me greatly in just about every other aspect of my life. I've enjoyed almost every moment of it, too – even the hard times were rewarding in one way or another.

I served my time the tough way, without any short cuts. But these days there are plenty of opportunities to improve your skills a little less painfully. A lot more is known about causes and effects: training methods, technique, tactics, nutrition and psychology are all understood much better, which is great for aspiring riders. So much of that painful trial and error can be avoided by learning from the experiences of people such as myself and from the many experts out there.

I hope that you will read and take note of the contents of this book: it might just steer you along the road towards improving your all-round cycling skills and knowledge, making everything that bit more enjoyable, not to mention helping you to go that little bit faster, and maybe even bringing you closer to personal victory.

See you up the road.

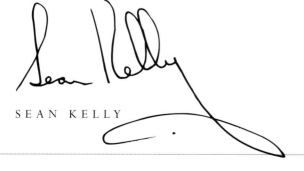

SEAN KELLY

Sean Kelly ranks as one of the all-time greats of road racing. His honours include:

Four wins in Tour de France points competition (record) 1982, 1983, 1985, 1989

Seven consecutive wins in Paris–Nice race 1982–1988

Overall winner of Vuelta a España 1988

Winner of Paris–Roubaix 1984, 1986

Winner of Tour of Lombardy, 1983, 1985, 1991

Winner of Liège–Bastogne–Liège 1984, 1989

Winner of Milan–San Remo 1986, 1992

Winner of Tour of Switzerland 1983, 1990

Winner of Grand Prix Des Nations 1986

Winner of Criterium Internationale 1983, 1984, 1987

Winner of Creteil–Chaville Classic 1984 (Paris–Tours)

Introduction

Years of personal experience on the part of the authors, together with advice from some of the world's top riders, trainers, physiologists and mechanics have gone into the following pages, making *The Racing Bike Book* a complete and thorough guide to all aspects of cycle racing. Written in a straightforward, no-nonsense style, with the minimum of jargon and technical terms, it should prove invaluable to anyone who is hoping to take up this great sport.

The first section of the book covers just about everything you need to know about bike racing: its disciplines, its heroes and its history. It also provides detailed explanations of techniques for competing in every area of the sport, setting you on the road to success.

The training section – the core of the book – gives tried and tested advice on how to get the most from your body. There is information on everything from nutrition to massage, including how to plan specific training schedules for your chosen event.

Finally, there is a down-to-earth guide to the essential hardware: the bike. However fit and tactically aware you are, unsuitable or poorly maintained equipment could cost you a race, so this section, which complements the earlier chapters, shows you how to choose your kit and how to make sure it is in perfect working order.

In short, the aim of *The Racing Bike Book* is to save you a great deal of the pain, time and trouble that will undoubtedly be a feature of your first few years of racing. Read it, trust it and learn from it: it should help you to have a faster and more enjoyable ride to a great cycling future. The rest is up to you.

Steve Thomas

The world of racing

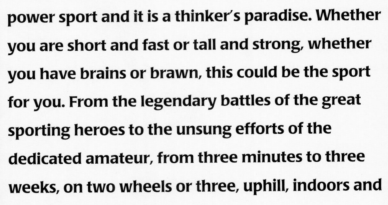

Welcome to the wonderful world of bike racing. This graceful, noble sport, with its many forms, has something to offer just about everyone. It is a team sport, it is an individual sport, it is a blood-and-guts power sport and it is a thinker's paradise. Whether you are short and fast or tall and strong, whether you have brains or brawn, this could be the sport for you. From the legendary battles of the great sporting heroes to the unsung efforts of the dedicated amateur, from three minutes to three weeks, on two wheels or three, uphill, indoors and even on grass, there is something about bike racing that draws people in and holds them for ever. Whatever you are looking for, you will find it somewhere down the road.

The great tours

The three major national tours are marathon, multi-week stage races for elite professional riders. The duration of these great races and the extreme conditions are unparalleled in almost any other sport. They test the riders' all-round abilities to the full and push them to the limit. Simply finishing one of these events is an achievement, while to win a single stage can make a rider a national hero. Overall victory in one of the great tours is the ambition of every bike racer, but is achieved by only a select few.

The Tour de France is the greatest bike race on earth, and the biggest annual sporting event on the planet. '*La Grande Boucle*', as the Tour is known, is the undoubted jewel in the crown of bike racing. From its beginnings in 1903, the Tour has evolved into a gruelling three-week epic. The leader's *maillot jaune* (yellow jersey) has become the most treasured prize in cycling.

In the midst of the July heat, the riders race well in excess of 100 miles (160km) each day, covering much of France and usually a couple of other countries on the way. The racing is fast and hard: the *crème de la crème* of cyclists line up at the start in the hope of inscribing their names into the history books. The Alps and the Pyrenees provide the most dramatic battlegrounds, and many competitors fall by the wayside before the welcome sight of the Eiffel Tower and the finish on the Champs Elysées in Paris.

The Giro D'Italia

The Giro, as the Tour of Italy is known, takes place in May–June, and is often used as a training ground or test bed for many Tour de France contenders. Although arguably the

second of the big tours, it is certainly not inferior in quality, and many riders now choose either the Tour or the Giro as their season's main target. The importance of the race in Italy is phenomenal, and

ABOVE: The Giro d'Italia race leader in time trial action.

RIGHT: The Eiffel Tower in Paris, the sight of which marks the end of three weeks of pain for Tour de France riders.

FAR RIGHT: The field in the Tour de Langkawi, the major Asian race.

the entire year you will find races ranging from two days to two weeks in length taking place not only in Europe but throughout the world.

For many European racers the season starts in late February with races all around the southern Mediterranean, such as the Ruta Del Sol and Vuelta a Murcia in Spain, Terreno–Adriatico and Tour of the Mediterranean in Italy, and then the Paris–Nice in March, the first serious race of the year.

As the weather warms up so does the racing, and just about every country in Europe now has at least one major stage race, which is often part of the Pro Tour calendar, the highest level of races in which the Pro Tour teams (cycling's elite teams) are obliged to compete.

The popularity of cycling is not just restricted to Europe; you will find major international, as well as regional, stage races all over the world. Many of the top pro riders from Europe start their seasons riding such races in Australia, Africa and Asia during the winter, a sure sign of the sport's growing globalisation.

every Italian professional racer puts a good Giro performance at the top of his season's hit list.

The race is very tough, with the Alps and Dolomites providing extreme terrain and weather to test the riders in their quest for the *maglia rosa*, the race leader's pink jersey.

The Tour of Spain

Traditionally, the Tour of Spain always took place during May, but it has now been moved to September to avoid any clash with the Giro. The race ranks just behind the Giro in prominence, but it is of equal proportions and as extreme in its demands. The Vuelta has always been recognised as a climber's tour, favouring the Spanish 'mountain goats', with big mountain-top finishes being a trademark of the race. The Vuelta rarely leaves Spain and often traverses much of the country.

Other major stage races

Stage racing is very much at the heart of professional cycling, and throughout

The classics

The so-called 'classics' are single-day races, many of which have been run virtually every year almost since cycle racing began. Each has its own individual characteristics and is held over more or less the same route each year. Most of these events form part of the World Cup series; they are high-profile races which every professional cyclist would like to win.

Most of the major classics are held in northern Europe during the spring, while others take place towards the end of the season, when the big tours are over. However, few modern riders seem to be able to perform in both the tours and the classics. The following is a selection of the most famous single-day races.

Milan–San Remo, held in March, is the first major classic of the year. Part of the course follows the very hilly, windy coast road along the Italian Riviera. The race is always hard and fast, with the winning attack usually taking place on the Poggio, the last climb, which is followed by a steep descent right into the finish.

The Tour of Flanders is centred around the hilly western region of Flanders, in Belgium, and takes place during early April. The race is renowned for its all-too-numerous short, steep, cobbled hills, called *murs*, and endless rough-surfaced farm tracks. This is without doubt one of the toughest classic races, and one of the most prestigious to win, especially as Flanders has always been one of the centres of European road racing.

Paris–Roubaix is perhaps the hardest single-day bike race in the world. It is run over more than 150 miles (240km) from Compiègne, north of Paris, to Roubaix, where it finishes on the velodrome. The tough bit is the terrain: although the race is fairly flat, the course includes some 25 or so short sections of *pavé*, or cobbled track. These are extremely rough,

TOP: *The Tour of Lombardy.*
ABOVE: *A rider fights his way up one of the cobbled* murs *in the Tour of Flanders.*

even by farm-track standards, and shake the riders and their bikes to pieces. When you consider also that it often rains for this April race, it is obvious why Paris–Roubaix is the most feared and prized classic of them all.

Paris–Roubaix, the 'Queen of the Classics': flat, open, cobbled hell for most of the riders. **LEFT:** *Milan–San Remo winds its way along the windswept Mediterranean coastline for much of its route.*

Contrary to what one might expect in a Dutch race, the course is quite hilly. Held towards the end of April, it is always seen as the last chance for a spring classic win by top riders who have missed out.

The Tour of Lombardy in northern Italy is known as 'the race of the falling leaves', as it is the last important classic race of the season, in October. It is always hard fought by riders trying to secure vital points in the World Cup competition or striving to secure a contract for the following season.

Liège–Bastogne–Liège is the oldest classic on the calendar, and one of the hilliest. It takes place in April in the Belgian Ardennes, which are renowned for their many steep hills; the race seems to take in every one of these *murs*, one after another, making it a real strong man's classic.

The Amstel Gold Race is a relative baby, being just over 20 years old. But as the only major race held in the Netherlands, a nation that is particularly cycling-orientated, it has quickly become one of the classics.

Modern heroes

There have been many top-class riders throughout cycling history, whose character, style, determination and results all go towards making them great. We could dedicate a whole book to famous racers and not even touch upon many of the heroes of the road, but instead we have chosen to shine the spotlight on some of the greats from the last 30 years.

Eddy Merckx, from Belgium, was the first of the all-time heroes of modern cycling history. 'The Cannibal', as he was known, certainly ranks as the greatest bike racer the world has yet seen, and looks set to retain that status. During his reign in the 1970s, he dominated professional cycling in a totally unforgiving fashion. From becoming the youngest ever amateur

Eddy Merckx. RIGHT: *Bernard Hinault.*
ABOVE RIGHT: *Greg LeMond.*

world champion at just nineteen, he went on to victory in five Tours de France and won almost everything else there was to win, achieving far more than any other rider before or since.

Then, the Frenchman Bernard Hinault took over the champion's reins, winning five Tours de France, along with other major stage races, the World Championships and a host of classics in the early 1980s. He was the last of the truly dominant winners of the Tour.

The gentle giant Miguel Indurain of Spain became the next member of the five Tours winners' club, dominating the race with his amazing time trial ability and consistent wisdom. Indurain (with a resting heart rate of 21bpm) changed the style of Tour racing, and looked set to be last of the great five-timers – until recently, that is.

Recovering miraculously from testicular cancer, American Lance Armstrong returned to competition in

Roche, who took the Tour, Giro and World Championship triple in 1987.

The last great climber to win the Tour was Italian Marco Pantani, a diminutive shaven-headed mountain goat, who is sadly no longer with us but remains one of the most charismatic racers of all time.

Many of the great tour champions have also been good single-day riders, but the true classics riders remain a breed of their own. In recent years Ireland's Sean Kelly, Belgium's Johan Musseuw and Italian Paolo Bettini have

ABOVE LEFT: *Lance Armstrong.*
FAR LEFT: *Miguel Indurain.*
LEFT: *Johan Musseuw.* ABOVE: *Jeannie Longo.*

been amongst the most successful, showing amazing versatility in the variable single-day epics.

In recent years the women's professional scene has really taken off, especially in the USA and Europe. One of the most accomplished riders ever is Jeannie Longo of France, who has won just about everything in the sport during her 20-plus years at the top. Even into her late 40s she is still winning major races.

And as the ink dries on these pages many new young contenders will be making their stamp on the sport, and more and more of these are emerging from non-European countries, spreading the sport far and wide.

1999, against all odds. The amazing American focused purely on the Tour de France, and won the event a record-breaking seven straight times before retiring undefeated in 2005 and becoming the most iconic cyclist of all time.

In between these dominant reigns several other great champions made their mark on the grand tours. Greg Lemond of the USA won the Tour de France three times, the first non-European to do so. His archrival was Frenchman Laurent Fignion, a double Tour winner. Ireland also had its share of the laurels thanks to Stephen

Cyclo-cross and triathlon

Slightly apart from the mainstream racing scene are cyclo-cross and triathlon, both of which originated in road and track racing but have since gone their separate ways, developing their own culture and traditions.

Cyclo-cross, in which riders race cross-country on adapted road bikes, has been around for most of this century. Originally, it was seen simply as a method for road and track racers to keep fit and competitive during the traditional winter close season. In those early days, riders would usually use single- or fixed-gear bikes, and would often compete against runners.

The winter sport of cyclo-cross is fast, gruelling and usually very muddy.

During the 1950s, the sport began to grow in prominence and duly earned World Championship status. This, inevitably, encouraged the development of special bikes and equipment, and ultimately specialist cyclo-cross riders emerged. Since then, the sport has gone from strength to strength, and it now has a World Cup competition and a busy international calendar, with Belgium and Holland being the most fanatical 'cross nations. The season runs from September through to February.

Triathlons

Triathlons are not strictly speaking cycling events, but since one third of the 'tri' discipline is cycling the sport has definite links with cycle racing,

and with time trialling in particular. Several top riders have come to road racing via triathlon, including the American Champion Lance Armstrong. The sport originated in the USA in the mid 1970s; it has grown dramatically since then, and is now an Olympic discipline.

A classic triathlon starts with a swimming race, moves straight into the cycling, and then finishes with a run. The distances vary considerably: sprint events start with a 400-metre swim (often indoors), followed by a twelve-mile (20km) bike ride, and finish with a three-mile (5km) road run. The classic Olympic distance

consists of a 1.5km swim, a 40km bike leg and a 10km run to finish. At the other end of the scale is the Ironman, a gruelling event that originated in Hawaii, which starts with a 4,800-metre sea swim, moves on to a 112-mile (180km) bike ride and finishes with a full 26-mile (42.2km) marathon.

Increasingly popular are duathlons; these are run–bike–run events, which are often favoured by land-loving cyclists. Distances in these events vary considerably.

Triathlons and duathlons do undoubtedly require a high level of fitness, but competitors of all abilities take part. As a cyclist, you will have the advantage of being pretty fit anyway, and also of having a third of the discipline already under control.

RIDING CYCLO-CROSS

Cyclo-cross races are friendly and informal, with riders of all ages and abilities competing on all kinds of bikes. Most races can be entered 'on the line' (on the day), and they are often run on a massed-start, multi-category basis. The standard race lasts one hour, and races are usually held on a circuit of between half a mile and two miles (1–3km) in distance. Courses vary dramatically: some are fast, flat grass circuits, where it is possible to ride all the way round, whilst others are slow and muddy and demand a lot of running.

ABOVE: *The Ironman is the toughest of them all.*
LEFT: *Competitors swap between bikes, running shoes and wetsuits in the transition area.*

Extremes

There is a lot more happening on two wheels than just the mainstream disciplines with which we are all familiar. There are a large number of 'cult' or 'extreme' forms of bike racing: some are strange, but all are interesting, and all go to make up the rich tapestry of this great sport.

With the majestic feel of an ancient jousting tournament, grass-track racing is like something from another era. Riders compete on track bikes with lower gearing and studded tyres, and in many ways the meetings resemble ordinary 'hard' track meetings, except that they take place on unbanked, rough and bumpy grass tracks.

The racing is fast, rough and exciting, and is usually based on a handicap system. Most events take place at fetes or festivals. In Scotland, the sport's ancestral home, the racing forms an important part of many highland games meetings, with a whole breed of unofficial grass-track professionals competing, and with gambling on races being common.

Speed records

The current cycling land speed record holder, with a record of 167.5 miles per hour (268km/h) set in 1995, is Dutchman Fred Rompelberg, who is also the world's oldest professional. Speed records are big-budget affairs, with the rider being towed up to speed and then paced by a racing car with special fairings. Salt-lake flats and similar places play host to these record attempts. The gears used are horrifically big and often need complex pulley systems to work them, while the bikes are usually longer and well reinforced to cope with the stresses of reaching such high speeds.

The title of 'world's fastest cyclist' is precious, but the price is high: Rompelberg has broken virtually every bone in his body during his long quest for the record.

Hill climbs

Towards the end of the road-race season, certain mountainous areas, notably in Spain and Colombia, play host to massed-start hill-climb races. These events tend to go literally straight up a mountain, often involving over an hour's climbing – and nothing else.

In Britain, the season draws to a close with a series of individual hill-climb races. Riders are timed, time-trial style, up some of the country's steepest, toughest climbs. These events tend to last for only a few minutes, which makes them particularly intense.

Roller racing

A closet sport, rarely seen these days, roller racing is often used as an entertainment at festivals and charity

sport is a great crowd pleaser, as each competitor's progress can be seen easily without the rider or spectator leaving the room.

Trikes and tandems

Racing is not restricted to standard road bikes, either. Tandems are regularly seen in time trials and in track sprint races, and even sometimes in special tandem road races.

The sight of a trike race is amazing: although trike riders usually stick to time trialling, they also occasionally appear in grass-track events and even in massed-start criteriums. Racers hurtle around corners on two wheels, hanging off the side of their machines, almost like competitors in a Roman chariot race.

Relays

Although it is a declining sport, a small number of relay races still take place. The most famous of them all is the 'Little 500', contested in Minneapolis, USA, where local college teams race 500 laps of an athletics track on single-speed bikes. One bike is used by all the members of the team.

LEFT: *Dutch veteran Fred Rompelberg and his speed-record machine on the salt-lake flats.*
ABOVE: *A British rider gives his all on a short, three-minute hill climb.*
RIGHT: *Tandem racing is fast and furious, but nowadays most tandems are ridden competitively only in time trials.*

events. Riders race on free rollers linked to a large clock, which shows the equivalent road distance covered.

Usually, four riders race at a time, with the aim being to get their arrow, or hand, around the clock first. The

CHAPTER 2

Road racing

Road racing has many forms, some of which may not suit

you, your likes and dislikes, your physical capabilities or your ambitions. This chapter will help you to choose which

types of event are best for you. Whatever kind of race you ultimately find yourself riding, it will not only call on great physical strength but will also demand a high level of skill and tactical knowledge. These attributes are usually gained only through years of experience, some of which may be painful; the second aim

of this chapter, therefore, is to help you avoid some of that pain by giving you an understanding of the most important techniques that you will need to survive and prosper in races.

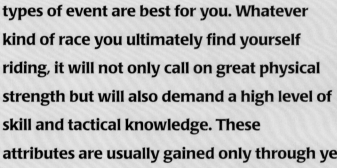

Types of road race

The term 'road race' is very broad; there are actually several different kinds of road race, some of which suit certain kinds of riders more than others, and some of which are peculiar to certain countries.

A 'road race' as such is usually a single-day, massed-start race. The classics, such as Paris–Roubaix, are usually run from place to place, but the vast majority of road races are held on circuits which are covered several times. Distances vary, depending on the race category, but can be anywhere between 30 and 150 miles (50–240km).

These events form the backbone of racing in most countries, and usually offer distances, terrains and degrees of difficulty for just about everyone.

Stage races

Races that continue over several days are known as stage races. From three-week events such as the Tour de France to local stage races run over long weekends, their aim is to test the all-round strengths of the riders. They often have a time-trial stage, along with hilly and flat road stages. There is a great deal of honour in winning each day's stage, but the rider who has the lowest total time for the race is the overall victor.

Most international stage races are either all-professional or open to elite 'amateur' teams, whereas local stage races are usually for amateurs only.

Criteriums

These are short, fast races, usually lasting between one and two hours, held on small, closed circuits a mile

or so around. They often take place in town centres as part of a festival. Many European towns have their own criterium, and often the local professional rides to please the home fans.

Fast and furious racing is always guaranteed, with primes (intermediate lap prizes) usually being awarded every lap or two to spice things up.

Many criteriums are actually decided on a points basis, the points going to the first few riders across the line on predetermined laps of the race.

Particularly popular in France are 'nocturnes', criteriums held in the dark – although usually on illuminated roads. These are quite spectacular and atmospheric to watch.

ABOVE: *The green, polka-dot, yellow and white leaders jerseys in the Tour de France. Points, mountains, overall and young rider leaders respectively.*
TOP LEFT: *Most place-to-place road races are large-scale affairs for elite amateur and/or professional riders.*
LEFT: *High-speed city-centre action, typical of a criterium race. Criteriums are very popular in northern Europe, where massive crowds turn out to watch the action.*
RIGHT: *Most amateur road races, like this one, cover a number of laps of a circuit.*

••••••••••••••••••••••••••••••••••

Kermesses

A kermesse is a cross between a road race and a criterium. These events form the mainstay of Belgian racing and are noted for being especially tough. They are usually held over distances of between 50 and 75 miles (80–120km), on fairly flat road circuits of between three and six miles (5–10km) in length, with primes on most laps. Many aspiring young riders survive on money won in these events, which ensures that the racing is always particularly fast.

Handicap or Australian pursuit races

Held on the road or on a closed circuit and usually about 30 to 50 miles (50–80km) in distance, these events are run on a handicap basis, with the riders starting in groups at different times according to age, sex, category or ability. For example, a group of veteran men may set off two minutes behind the women's group, and five minutes in front of

the elite group. The idea is that the whole race should come together for the finish, but that of course depends on just how well the riders in each group work together. These events are particularly popular as early-season training races, owing to the need for a constant high level of power output.

Semi-competitive riding

If out-and-out racing is a bit too serious, or simply not what you are after, there are alternatives, where it is up to you just how hard you push yourself – or not, as the case may be. Not only are *randonnée* events useful as training, even for the best riders, but they also provide a great introduction to competition for aspiring racers, allowing them to learn the many skills required to compete successfully without too much pressure and without the need to have a licence and all the latest kit.

In recent years mass participation events have really taken off, and you'll now find hundreds of them all over the world, and thousands of cyclists of every level and ability lining up to take part.

The best known is L'Etape du Tour. This is an annual 'race' for ordinary cyclists along a classic stage of the Tour de France. Around 8,000 riders take part annually, ranging from top professional and amateur racers to weekend cyclists. Closed roads, support vehicles and all of the frills you'd expect from the Tour itself can be experienced.

Many of the classic races in Europe have such mass participation versions, giving you the chance to follow in the wheel-marks of the top pros, and in many cases even have the chance to ride along with them. Even some stage races, such as the Tours of Germany and Austria, have multi-day versions so that you can get to feel what it's like to ride one.

The biggest of these events is the Cape Argus Tour, held annually around Cape Town, where around

ABOVE RIGHT: *The Etape du Tour is the most famous cyclo sportive.*
RIGHT: *Competitors in the Ardechoise event.*

35,000 riders compete. Europe's biggest event is the L'Ardechoise, held each June in the French Ardech region, with various distance options available for the 15,000 competitors.

Audax

Audax events are held over distances of anything between 60 and 750 miles (100–1,200km), and are ridden as

near to non-stop as possible, the aim being to reach a set standard time. These events are good endurance training but are increasingly popular in their own right as a way of testing oneself in a friendly not too-competitive environment. Every four years the legendary Paris–Brest–Paris Audax, 750 miles (1,200km) in length, attracts thousands of riders from all over the world. It is the 'Olympics' of the Audax world. To qualify for this it is necessary to complete a series of tough qualifying events at varying distances.

Permanent *randonnées*

There are also a number of 'permanent *randonnées*', routes that you can go and ride when you please. You must first pre-register with the organising club; they supply you with a control card, which you have stamped along the route to prove that you have completed the ride. Afterwards, you send in the card and receive a medal or certificate to confirm your achievement.

Some of these *randonnées* have become classic challenges: the Raid Pyrénéen, for example, is one of the great permanent *randonnées*, running across the Pyrenees from Hendaye on the Atlantic coast to Cerbère on the Mediterranean. Riders climb all the major mountains of the Tour de France on the way, with the aim being to complete the 446 miles (714km) within 100 hours.

The Raid Pyrénéen attracts riders from all over the world, who take up the challenge of riding from coast to coast across the backbone of the Pyrenees. Each rider receives his or her own frame number to attach to the bike.
LEFT AND BELOW: Randonnées *can cover all sorts of terrain. A* randonnée *may be a highly sociable event, or very solitary.*

Bunch riding skills

It takes a great deal of skill, nerve and knowledge to ride in a big road-race bunch. But once you have mastered the necessary techniques you will have a much easier and far more successful race.

The main principle involved in bunch riding is slipstreaming: you use far less energy when riding in the shelter of one or more other riders. Your priorities in a race are to conserve as much energy as possible for when you need it most, and at the same time to keep yourself safe and in contention. The first rule is to avoid the rear end of a bunch: not only do you get a harder ride, but there is a greater risk of crashes. Equally, try not to ride on the front whenever possible, since you will be putting in a greater effort and using up vital energy that you may need later. The ideal position is in the first quarter of the bunch – out of trouble and out of the wind, but in contention.

On the flat in particular, wind is always the biggest problem, and this is where you need to start using your head: be aware that twists and turns in the road will alter the direction of the wind and consequently where you need to ride. Try to seek shelter at all times, staying somewhere in the middle of the group. When a bunch is riding hard into the wind, echelons inevitably form at the front (see photograph below); if you are not near the front in an echelon, you will be forced to ride without shelter 'in the gutter', where it is twice as hard, and you may get dropped. In windy sections of a race, force your way up towards the front of the bunch: even if it means a short spell of solo riding into the wind to get there, it will pay off.

Uphill

Whether you can climb well or not, you should aim to be near the front on hills, so that you stay in

Echelons are formed to combat the wind: riders form a line across the road so that each is protected from the wind by the person in front and only the front rider is exposed. They then take turns to ride at the front, dropping backwards on the sheltered side. Any rider who slips out of line will be in the wind and in trouble.

contention when the inevitable pressure goes on: if you start to suffer, you will be able to drift back slowly through the bunch instead of simply getting dropped. On a short climb, stay with the bunch at all costs; on longer climbs, try and ride at your own pace, limiting your losses as far as possible. However, try not to find yourself on your own, as it will be difficult to get back to the bunch. (See also pages 30–1.)

Down and around

On descents and on short fast circuits, you should aim to stay well to the front of the bunch: it may be hard to get up there, but the ride will be much easier than it would be towards the rear. You not only remain in contention, you stay out of danger. (See also pages 32–5.)

ABOVE: *Staying relaxed and aware is vital.*
BELOW: *A lack of concentration can leave you on the floor.*

(See also pages 30–1.)

ETIQUETTE AND PRINCIPLES

1 **Stay relaxed but aware: do not tense up and touch your brakes too hard.**
2 **Be courteous to your fellow riders by giving them room and looking around before changing your position.**
3 **Never cut inside other riders on corners.**
4 **When the pressure goes on, fight to hold your place. You will have to be firm: any sign of weakness and you will find yourself 'off the back'.**
5 **It is frowned upon to attack through feeding zones or when crashes occur.**
6 **In a large bunch sprint, the safest place is near the front, just behind the riders who are fighting it out.**

Tactics

In a bike race, the good guy does not always win, but the wise guy usually does. While there is no substitute for a big heart and a good pair of legs, if you do not have a good tactical sense they will not get you very far. Brains all so often win out over brawn on the road. The following are key tactics that you need in order to survive and prosper.

If you want to be successful in road races, knowing exactly when, where and how to attack is crucial. First, you need to determine your motives: there is simply no point in wasting energy attacking for the sake of it. You have to decide whether you intend to go it alone to win, or to force other riders to come with you, maybe getting rid of any hangers-on from the back of the group. Once you have made a realistic choice, you need to decide when and where to attack.

This will depend both on the state of play on the road and on your own physical state: you have to be sure that you have the energy to carry out the attack successfully. If you are 30 miles from the finish, the others are looking strong and you are on a wide, open road, then you are wasting your time.

Headwinds and straight, flat roads are not conducive to breakaways. Narrow, twisty roads, descents, bad weather, tailwinds and towns are.

The next question is when: basically, you have to have an element of surprise, and to be at a point where other riders may hesitate to respond. Right over the crest of a hill or going into a corner are classic times to attack. In the closing stages of a race, if you think you cannot win the sprint, an attack within the last half-mile or so will almost certainly result in a hesitant chase.

When you do intend to attack, do

not announce it to everyone: discreetly manoeuvre yourself into a position where you cannot be easily seen by the first few riders in the bunch, quietly get into gear and attack flat out on the opposite side of the road, not looking around for at least ten seconds.

Self-preservation

Always be ready to respond to any interesting-looking attacks: a rider who starts to look edgy, tightens up his or her shoes, changes gear and looks around a couple of times may

ABOVE: *A rider assesses the state of play before deciding whether or not to attack this small leading group.*
TOP: *Here, a rider gives his all in a solo attack, although a wide, open road is not the best place to make a move.*

well be about to put in an attack. If you know this is a good rider, or the time is right, prepare to follow.

On a climb, if you hear the click of gears and sense that someone is about to attack from behind you, a slight sideways move could well deter him or her for the moment. Never show that you're suffering on a climb if you are, just stay out of sight when your tongue is hanging out.

If you find yourself in a small group nearing the finish, think ahead. Make sure that you are following someone who is a 'soft pedaller', so that you do not have to put in too much effort to get past, and try to avoid having the fastest rider right on your wheel and giving him or her the perfect lead-out. A grimace or two could enable you to miss a few vital turns on the front, allowing you to manoeuvre yourself discreetly into the best position, one from which you can both watch and respond.

Conversely, just speeding up a touch and looking calm as someone tries to come through off your wheel can be quite intimidating.

KEY TACTICS

1 **Always play your cards close to your chest. Never show how you feel, unless you are pretending to be tired in order to avoid riding at the front.**
2 **Confidence and aggression can often intimidate other riders, so use them, within reason, to get your own way. You may have to be ruthless to save your own skin.**
3 **Always know your opposition. Find out who can sprint or climb well, and who always exhausts him or herself with pointless moves, and use that knowledge to monitor their movements.**
4 **Be aware of club alliances and rider friendships. Certain riders will never chase others; some will chase enemies, even club-mates, at any cost, just to prevent their success. Choose your breakaway partners carefully.**
5 **In breakaway situations, think carefully before trying to drop your companions. You may be able to lose them uphill, but they could help you a great deal on the flat: it is not always a clear-cut situation.**

The rider in front is using up his strength, while the man behind him is taking it easy and waiting to attack.
LEFT: *Riders with a common aim work together to share the pace and give one another shelter in order to catch the group in front.*

Climbing

When the road goes up, the going gets tough. Hills, essentially, are where races are won – and lost, for that matter. Improving your climbing is vital if you want to improve your performance.

Hills can be divided into two basic types: power climbs, which are the short, steep kind, and endurance climbs, the longer, often high-altitude variety. It used to be said that climbers were small and skinny, but tall, powerful riders such as Indurain and Merckx have proved that almost anyone can climb hills quickly. It is also quite simple to improve your climbing: fitness is the crucial factor, although there is, of course, a great deal more to it.

Power climbs

Power climbs are generally not long enough to call heavily on endurance: they tend to demand power and strength. These climbs are best approached in a fairly high gear and 'attacked' out of the saddle. In this position, power comes mainly from the lower back and the thighs, with a bracing effect coming from the upper body through the arms. You should avoid straining too heavily on the bars and throwing your bike around, however, as this just wastes energy. It is also important to use your leg muscles fully on such climbs, pushing down and pulling up right through the pedal stroke to create a smooth, efficient action.

Within a race, it is best to ride such climbs near to the front of the group, and to fight to stay within it at all costs. Be aware, too, that attacks

A steady, regulated effort is needed for longer mountain climbs, such as those seen in the great tours.

often come just over the summit, so you should select a gear in which you can react.

Endurance climbs

Longer climbs, such as those you see in the Alps, call far more on fitness and endurance than do power climbs.

POWER CLIMBING ❶ The majority of the power is coming from the lower back and through the thighs. ❷ The upper body is tensed to brace this power and to ensure efficiency, as the legs are both pushing and pulling in a near-perfect circular action. ❸ The rider's body weight is kept low and back over the saddle to ensure that the large gear being used does not jerk and cause a loss of traction.

CLIMBING TECHNIQUES

1 **Think positive, do not be afraid, and stay calm whenever possible.**

2 **The less weight you carry the better: light tyres, empty bottles and so on all help.**

3 **Think ahead with your gearing: do not leave it until you are straining.**

4 **If it is wet or gritty, be sure to keep your weight over the rear wheel when riding out of the saddle.**

5 **On longer climbs, always be prepared for cold and wet weather over the top, and put on a cape and hat before descending.**

The correct pace and power output are the most important factors. You should always aim to ride these climbs at a pace that you feel you can comfortably sustain for the duration of the climb: your own ideal speed can be learned only through experience. Essentially, it should be steady: use a gear that allows you to pedal comfortably and smoothly, getting out of the saddle only occasionally. When you do, it is important that you are not straining with your upper body: all your power should be coming from below your waist. You also need to be very aware of your breathing, and to concentrate on taking deep, regular breaths.

In a race, the nearer to the front of the group you are the better on long climbs, as you will then be able to

All-out power climbing is sustainable only for short periods of time.

drift back if you need to, or even dictate the pace. Advance knowledge of a climb is very useful both tactically and for pacing yourself, but do not think too much about how hard it is going to be, or you will destroy your morale and suffer twice as much.

ENDURANCE CLIMBING ❶ The rider is sitting well back in the saddle, with his lower back and thighs creating a smooth, efficient pedalling action. ❷ The upper body is relaxed, with the hands on the top of the bars, relieving the back and allowing for unrestricted breathing. ❸ Riding out of the saddle is used only to maintain a rhythm and to rest aching back muscles, and should be very smooth, with very little straining in the upper body.

Descending

Minutes can be gained by good descenders on long downhill stretches, with no extra physical effort – just skill and concentration. This is an area in which it is easy to achieve improvements, as it is mostly a question of confidence.

For some unknown reason, the art of descending is one aspect of cycling to which riders rarely pay much attention. Yet you only need to watch the Tour de France to see its importance. It is all very well being able to climb efficiently, but if you cannot get down the other side both quickly and safely you will have wasted all that effort.

Long descents, such as you see in the Tour, call heavily on aerodynamics. The first thing, therefore, is to attain an efficient, aerodynamic body position. (Do not, however, try to imitate those you see on television. The top

professionals have the benefit of clear, closed roads, lead motorbikes and years of experience.) In order to reduce head-on wind resistance, you should crouch low over the bars, but not so low as to restrict your forward vision.

Your elbows should be tucked well in, with your hands on the drops; the pedals should be horizontal and your knees pointing inwards, and your backside should be positioned well to the back of your saddle.

Throughout the descent, you must be totally focused on the job and completely aware of what is going on around you. Use your ears to tell you when riders or vehicles are approaching from behind, and watch shadows to the side; keep an eye on the road a bend or two down the valley, as reaction time is limited when you are moving at this kind of speed.

The correct line is also very important, especially on shorter, more technical descents. Firstly, it must be safe, which means that you should stay on the right side of the road unless you can see a long way ahead. Paint on the road and roadside grit should also be avoided. You should plan how to line up for corners as far in advance as you

DESCENDING ❶ The rider's line is near the centre of the road, where it is both smooth and direct whilst allowing movement to either side if necessary. ❷ As he reaches the corner, the fastest and straightest line through is plotted, and his weight is pushed back on the saddle. ❸ You can see how he is crouched low over the bike, reducing head-on wind resistance.

SAFE DESCENDING

1 Leave plenty of space between you and other riders, avoiding nervy riders.

2 If you do not know a descent, try following someone sensible who does.

3 Always wear track mitts, and keep your chest warm.

4 Make sure drinking bottles, pumps and so on are secure before you descend.

5 Stop pedalling only when the pedals are spinning so fast they give you nothing to brace against, and you bounce around in the saddle.

can, choosing the classic racing line — as direct as is safely possible (see pages 34–5) — and being careful not to oversteer on hairpin bends.

Brake well ahead, and right into the corner. Also be aware that on longer climbs rims heat up and brakes become less efficient, so a 'feathering' brake action well before the bend may be necessary. In wet conditions, allow a 50 per cent greater braking distance, and do not brake on wet bends. Before entering the corner, also think ahead to the exit, changing down a gear if necessary.

The best way to improve your descending is to go downhill a little

An aerodynamic position will make a massive difference to your speed on a long descent. Use a full aero tuck only when the road is clear and you can see well ahead to plot a safe line.

faster in training: otherwise you will never find your limits! Try easing off the brakes more than usual, experiment with lines and positions, concentrate on thinking ahead all the time and stay relaxed.

❹ The legs and arms are well tucked in so as to reduce air turbulence, and the rider is seated well back, both to aid this process and to alter the centre of gravity for increased stability. ❺ The hands are on the drops, ready to react and brake when necessary. ❻ Pressure is put onto the outside pedal to alter the centre of gravity and to stabilise the bike.

Cornering

Cornering rapidly and effectively is truly an art, and one that it is essential to learn if you want to survive in the cut and thrust of a fast-moving peloton.

If you can perfect your 'line' and have the skill and confidence to corner well, you will find yourself staying both upright and near the head of affairs in a race, and when the going gets rough that will almost certainly make the difference between winning and simply finishing. The few metres gained or lost on that tight corner coming into the finishing straight of a criterium are some of the most vital of the race.

As long as you think logically, finding the correct 'line' to take on a corner is easier than it looks. The classic racing line is usually achieved by entering the corner wide, on the outside of the entry road, cutting in close to the apex of the bend and coming out of it on the far side of the exit road. Essentially, you are attempting to smooth out the bend by using the road to its maximum. Once you have attained the ideal line, you have to start learning to compromise, avoiding drains, road markings, grit and off-camber sections, and plotting two or three possible lines as you approach the corner.

Technique

As you come into a corner, and just before you start to brake, you should change down into a gear that will allow you to accelerate out of the other side. You should avoid braking until the last minute, and let the brakes off just as you start to lean in towards the corner.

When you enter a corner at speed, your hands should be on the 'drops', your outside pedal down and your weight pushed back on the saddle. As you start to turn, you should almost stand on your outside leg, forcing yourself slightly out of the saddle. Meanwhile, your inside knee and

CORNERING ❶ The rider enters the corner on the far outside line, just touching the brakes at the last moment and ❷ starting to lean into the bend.
❸ You can see how he is leaning into the bend with his knee and inside shoulder to give maximum traction, whilst also 'standing' on the outside pedal

··

CORNERING HINTS

1 Never corner faster than you know you can do safely.

2 In wet conditions, let a little air out of your tyres to improve traction.

3 If you can corner well, the entry to a corner is a great place to attack.

4 Look out for oil and diesel on corners, especially in city centres.

5 On chicanes or double bends, pick the best overall line, not just the best for the first corner.

6 Use sandpaper to remove the glossy finish from new tyres.

··

shoulder should be pointing slightly into the bend, as if to pull you through the corner. This effectively alters your centre of gravity and stabilises you, whilst allowing the bike to take its best line.

You can in fact pedal right through many corners, with practice, and this could gain you vital metres.

In a bunch situation, be aware of what is going on around you: do not get caught with someone unexpectedly on your inside. Hold your line by using the road and being positive, but always allow space for other people's errors. Although it is important to avoid being at the back of the bunch, respect etiquette and do not cut other riders up. Never test new equipment during a race on a twisty course. New forks, cranks, wheels or tyres may react very differently to your old ones on corners, so try them out first.

··

Cornering in a large bunch calls for a relaxed approach, fluidity and consideration for other riders. A small group can corner much more quickly than a large bunch. In either case the leading rider always has the easiest line.

to keep the bike upright. **❹** He hits the bend at the apex, lessening its angle. **❺** The exit line is a mirror image of the entry, keeping the angle shallow and the process smooth. **❻** As he exits, he sprints out of the saddle to regain speed.

Sprinting

The vast majority of races end in a sprint finish, be it a two-up sprint or a mass bunch finish. In a sprint, it is not always the fastest rider who wins: more often than not it is the cleverest. Sprinting demands explosive power and speed, but that has to be combined with confidence, a strong desire to win, sound tactics and perfect timing.

During the last few miles of a race, a good sprinter will build up a ruthless desire to win: the greater the desire, the greater the physical power the rider will generate. One way of doing this is to visualise the finish, always imagining yourself coming first: think third and you will be third at best. This single-mindedness is necessary to make sure that you get what you want, rather than becoming intimidated and finding yourself manipulated by other riders to do what they want. In short, you have to be harsh.

Sprinting demands a perfectly timed explosive physical effort: the aim is for the rider to 'get everything out' by the time the finish line is crossed. To do this effectively, you must know your strengths and use them. If you have a good last-minute

'kick', you should try to keep things slow until just before the line; if you have a long, fast turn of speed, go for a surprise early sprint. But always be sure that you time it right, and never

When a sprint is very close, a lunge may make all the difference.

find yourself jumping too early into a headwind that you did not expect.

SPRINTING ❶ Approaching the finish, the rider in red has made sure that he has the dual advantages of shelter from the wind and the element of surprise. ❷ As the rider in blue checks the position of the rider in red, the latter attacks on the 'open' side, using the element of surprise to gain vital distance. ❸ He begins an all-out sprint, explosive power coming from his thighs and lower back, with his arms and shoulders harnessing this power.

Tactics

In a large bunch sprint, fight at all costs to stay near to the front of the peloton, even if it means using extra energy to get there, and avoid getting blocked in – the sides of the bunch are most risky. Always be aware of lulls in speed, as they lead to regrouping of the bunch and attacks, so be prepared.

Find out exactly what the finish is like – ideally by seeing it beforehand, or if not by asking someone else. As you approach it, try to stay in the first ten, and hold back as other riders go too early, as they often do. If possible, follow a known fast man when he makes his move, and above all do not panic.

In a small group finish, the element of surprise is all-important. Stay at, or near, the rear of the group, keeping an eye out for riders who look strong. Be patient and do not get nervous, or you may end up following a fruitless attack. Move up towards the front only when you have almost reached flat-out speed. Above all, do not go for a long sprint unless you have a tailwind and you can gain a surprise gap and a good line.

SUCCESSFUL SPRINTING

1 Use your ears and watch out for the shadows of riders attacking from behind.
2 If there is a corner within the last 500 metres, make sure you are one of the first few riders round it.
3 Look for opportunities to catch other riders by surprise: when they are sitting down, changing gear or glancing sideways.
4 A flick of your elbow will often be enough to deter someone from trying to come past you or from pushing you out.
5 Always keep sprinting past the line, and lunge (throw) your bike forwards in the last couple of metres. Too many races are lost by not doing this.

Riders rarely sprint in a straight line. Bunch sprinting is hard at times, so beware and be prepared for any eventuality.

❹ As the rider in blue responds and tries to pass him on the inside, the rider in red narrows the gap in order to intimidate his opponent. ❺ Just metres from the finish line, it is neck and neck: a photo finish is in order. ❻ The rider in red steals victory with a finely timed lunge for the line, 'throwing' his bike over it to gain the vital half-wheel lead for victory.

Time trials and track racing

Although very different, these are perhaps the two purest forms of cycle racing. Time trials are true tests of speed, strength and determination: there is nowhere to hide, tactics are virtually non-existent, and anyone can

compete in them, no matter how fast or slow they may be. That said, there is a lot more to time trialling than pure brute strength.

Certain types of track race are solo tests, too, and have much in common with time trialling; conversely, some events

run on the track demand the ultimate in tactical awareness, while in others the main requirement is the ability to push and shove. One of the main attractions, perhaps, is that conditions are basically the same for everyone: one track, a fixed gear, no brakes and no external interruptions mean that track racing is cycling's equivalent of a 'level playing field'.

The race of truth

It is said that the time trial, the 'race of truth', spares nobody. There are no tactics: it is simply rider and machine against the clock. That makes it perhaps the purest and the toughest discipline within the sport of cycling.

It is not always true that the fittest rider wins a time trial. Being a good time triallist not only requires a high level of fitness, it makes huge mental demands. To race all alone against the clock, pushing yourself right to your limit from start to finish, requires immense determination and concent-ration and great strength of character. Even some of the greatest road riders of all time have not been able to perform well in time trials – some simply detest the pain of the discipline.

The purely physical demands of time trialling are so punishing because a competitor must ride at a constant pace, near to his or her maximum power output, for the duration of the event. If he or she rides below that pace, the race is lost; above it and there is a risk of 'blowing'. Self-knowledge is paramount.

Types of time trial

Time trials vary considerably in their duration and intensity, and in the importance that is attached to them.

In the UK, for example, they form the backbone of cycle racing: most events are held on fast main roads and are run over the standard distances of 10, 25, 50 and 100 miles (16, 40, 80 and 160km). Riders are generally more interested in their personal time than in winning.

In mainland Europe, however, time trials are not so prominent; they tend to be held on hilly, twisty circuits of varying lengths. Most international stage races also start with a short prologue time trial and have at least

ABOVE: *To be a successful time triallist, like Miguel Indurain, you need to be able to push yourself to the limit and to tolerate pain.*
LEFT AND ABOVE RIGHT: *Aerodynamic equipment and a smooth, efficient technique are all-important in a time trial, where every second counts.*
RIGHT: *Team time trials are often held during stage races. They are also run as separate events in their own right.*

one time-trial stage: over the past few years, this has been a decisive stage in races such as the Tour de France.

Technology

Aerodynamics, weight and efficiency are all vitally important when it comes to racing against the clock, and this has meant that time triallists have been willing to experiment with high-tech bikes, equipment and clothing. Changes began to occur in the mid 1980s, when equipment that had been developed for triathletes, such as low-

profile bikes and disc wheels, first started to appear in time trials. Then in 1989 the great American racer Greg LeMond dramatically gained overall victory in the Tour de France by a convincing win in the

final day's time trial, in which he was the only top contender using 'tri-bars'; this duly started a technological revolution.

Nowadays, even riders in low-key races have skin suits, aero helmets, tri-spoke wheels and tri-bars. (See pages 42–3, 104–5, 126–7, 136–7.) This equipment can save over a second per km and, other things being equal, can make the difference between first and second place – but remember, the time trial is the race of truth, and equipment will not help you without the commitment.

Go faster

If you are going to ride a good time trial, everything has to be spot on: your training, your preparation, your bike, your kit, your attitude and your speed.

The equipment that you use for a particular time trial will depend largely on the type of course and the terrain, and on what equipment you have at your disposal. The most important decisions you must make are, firstly, which bike to ride, for example, a low-profile is not much use up a mountain, and secondly, what

position. You can do this by looking at pictures or videos of yourself in action, but do not compromise too much on comfort. A skin suit and aero hat are also good low-cost investments, and a heart-rate monitor is invaluable for pacing yourself. (See Chapters 6, 7 and 8 for more advice on equipment and clothing.)

Anything that will help streamline the rider's body shape is worthwhile.
LEFT: The prologue time trial of the Tour de France usually has little bearing on the overall result, but it does determine who wears the first leader's yellow jersey.
RIGHT: Lance Armstrong demonstrates the use of aerobars to reduce the aerodynamic drag of his body.
BELOW RIGHT: With Aero wheels and helmet, a low-profile frame and tri-bars this rider is fully kitted out for going his fastest.

gear ratios to use (see pages 112–3). After that, the prime factors are weight and aerodynamics, the most important factor of all. Tri-bars are almost always beneficial, unless the course is all uphill, but for them to be really effective you should work on attaining an efficient, aerodynamic

The final countdown

It is crucial to arrive at the start of a time trial fully prepared, both physically and mentally. This usually means at least 20 minutes' warm-up, towards the end of which you will hit race pace. During this time, you need to concentrate on the race to come,

visualising yourself riding your best ever time trial and realising what you will have to do to accomplish that.

Always know exactly when you are due to start, and arrive at the line with about two minutes to go: this should not cause you to cool down too much, and gives you time to make final preparations. As you roll up to the start line, you should be in the right gear to accelerate away swiftly, and during the final 30 seconds you should be focusing totally on making a good start, and breathing deeply and calmly.

The sooner you can get up to speed the better, particularly in a

short event, but be aware that for a short while after the effort of the start you may have to ease up a little; if you don't 'overcook' the initial pace, your legs will soon recover.

In action

From your training rides you should have a good idea of what intensity you can sustain for the duration of the event (see Chapter 5); you should aim to keep your power output constant at that level, trying to avoid any major fluctuations of effort. If it drifts, you will lose time, so this is the main area

on which you should concentrate during the race.

In a time trial it is illegal to 'draught' or ride in the slipstream of other riders. However, you should

avoid the temptation to speed up to pass a rider you have caught; you are obviously going faster anyway, so do not exhaust yourself proving it. If another rider catches you before the last quarter of the race, do not try to keep up with him or her at a distance – you will just 'blow' – but in the last few miles you do not have too much to lose. The same theory can be applied if you are on your own: get everything out before the finish line, but do not blow before you reach the last few hundred metres. You will lose more time by doing that than you could possibly gain.

Long-distance time trialling

Although similar in some ways, long-distance time trialling is a quite different sport to traditional time trialling, involving unthinkable lengths of time and massive distances. Riders often subject themselves to extreme hardships, pushing their bodies and minds beyond their natural limits and sometimes losing any comprehension of what they are doing.

Long-distance time trials such as 12- and 24-hour events are particularly popular in the UK: the aim is to ride as far as possible, on a circuit, within the given period of time. Place-to-place record-breaking attempts are also common, with the 874-mile (1,400km) Land's End to John O'Groats record being the ultimate non-stop epic.

In the USA, there is the annual 3,000-mile (4,800km) Race Across America, or RAAM, which is not strictly speaking a time trial, but is effectively ridden as one. Riders start together but choose to ride at their own pace, and because of the extreme distance they soon become separated.

Equipment

For these events, comfort is more important than aerodynamics: riders tend to use more relaxed frame geometry and lower gear ratios (see pages 98–9, 110–11), along with comfortable riding positions and special features such as padded bars, fatter tyres and so on. Tri-bars are nearly always used, although often as much for comfort as for purposes of aerodynamics.

It is also important to use clothing that you find comfortable: genuine chamois, for example, is less likely to cause irritation than synthetic. Regular changes of undervests and wet clothes will keep you happy and avoid the risk of infection. When severe tiredness sets in, your body

The RAAM is a long, lonely ride and a supreme test of character and fitness.
RIGHT: *A rider takes a couple of minutes to eat and change clothing during a Land's End to John O'Groats record ride.*

• •

cools down very fast, so be sure to add plenty of extra layers.

Nutrition

The correct nutrition is crucial in marathon events. Depending on the weather conditions, you should aim to drink a bottle (550ml) of hydration and glucose polymer fluid every hour. Any food should be light and taken regularly. Although it is possible to rely on fluids alone, the mental benefit of eating something when you are near delirious after 24 hours in the saddle is immense, but anything that is likely to upset the by-now tender stomach should be avoided: this includes fats and sugars. Small

crustless sandwiches, not-too-sugary cakes and fruit are all morale-boosting treats. Heavy foods such as energy bars are best kept until they are really needed, or taken in small doses.

Riding long-distance events

A constant, even pace and a comfortable gear ratio are essential. The pace is best monitored by using a heart-rate monitor and should be adhered to strictly, until you get to the point where you cannot see the monitor!

This is the moment when your back-up crew really comes into play; following a predetermined plan, your helpers effectively take over your mind, making you eat, change your clothes or sleep for a few minutes if they feel it is needed, or putting you back on the bike if they judge that it is sensible to do so.

Rides such as these can be really hard on your mental state, but by thinking only about what you are doing at the moment, and about doing it well, you should stay fairly sane; if you think about how far you still have to go, it is all over. But you also have to know when to stop: going too far overboard could cause serious and permanent damage.

Types of track race

Track racing is fast and furious, often a contact sport and extremely exciting both to watch and to participate in. It is an excellent way of developing speed, power and bike-handling skills. Owing to the relative simplicity of the equipment needed to ride at a local level, it is also fairly cheap to do.

There is a whole range of different track events, and there is bound to be something to suit you, whatever your physical strengths. Races usually take place as part of a meeting, where riders compete in some or even all of the events.

The format of track meetings varies slightly, and will depend on the venue, the level of competition and the facilities available. But whether it is a six-day professional meeting or simply a local track league, you can expect to find many of the following events taking place.

Six-day racing is the winter showpiece of the professional track world. In the early days, riders would race non-stop for six whole days and nights, but now it is a little more civilised. Teams of two riders race on indoor city-centre tracks in a series of atmospheric late-night, multi-event track meetings.

Some events are effectively time trials run on the track, notably the pursuit, the blue riband event of track racing. Riders race individually against the clock, then head to head, with the fastest rider over the distance (usually 4,000 or 5,000 metres) being the victor. The team pursuit is run on the same format, with teams of four working together; the time is measured as the third rider crosses the line. The kilometre time trial is exactly as it sounds: the competitors, often sprinters, ride solo against the watch for a distance of one kilometre. It is one of the toughest events on the track. (See also pages 50–1.)

The sprint is generally 500 or 1,000 metres long, and is usually run head to head, in a knockout format. It is an extremely tactical and entertaining event, with the sprinting not usually starting in earnest until the last 300 metres.

The Olympic sprint is effectively a 1km time trial for teams of three

ABOVE: *Team sprint action.*
LEFT: *The Madison is effectively a rolling relay for two-man teams; the result is decided on points awarded on predetermined laps of the race.*

sprinters. One rider leads for a lap and then peels off the front, and then the second, and the third man finishes for the time.

An omnium is a compendium of events, usually a distance race, a sprint and a pursuit. Its aim is to find the best all-rounder.

The Madison is a race contested by teams of two riders. In effect, it is an ever-moving relay race. One rider must be racing at all times, whilst the other circles the track waiting to take over; the changeover is made, usually every two laps, by the faster rider 'slinging' the slower one into action. The results are decided by points gained on specific laps.

Some track events are run more in the style of massed-start road races: this is particularly true of distance races, which are of a set length, usually 10, 20 or 50 kilometres (6, 12 or 30 miles). These events are often contested by bunches of over 50 riders. A handicap race is usually run over a short set distance; between four and eight riders start from different 'marks' on the track, with the fastest man on the

TOP: *Riders fight for their positions as the lead motorbike winds up the pace in a kierin.*
ABOVE: *Sprint action at the highest level is fast, fierce and often brutal.*
RIGHT: *Late nights, loud music, alcohol and smoky arenas are all part of the entertaining six-day show.*

• •

'scratch' (furthest back) mark, and the winner is the first across the finish line. A points race is a distance race that is decided on the basis of points awarded to the leading riders across the line on predetermined laps.

One of the most entertaining events is the 'devil-take-the-hindmost', often known simply as the 'devil',

where the last rider across the line on each lap, or every few laps, is eliminated from the race. Usually, the last

four riders are left to contest the finish.

Finally, there are two races, the kierin and the motor-paced, where motorbikes are used to pace the riders. Originating in Japan, where it is a massive sport, the kierin is a short distance race where racers 'line out' in the slipstream of a motorbike, which winds the pace up and then leaves the riders to sprint out the last lap or two of the track. Racing is fast and aggressive. The motor-paced is a massed-start distance race where riders compete on specially constructed bikes and are paced by motorbikes for the entire event.

Track riding skills

Riding a fixed-wheel track bike on a banked track can be an intimidating prospect at first. True, it requires a certain amount of skill, but once you have developed the basic technique the whole process will become second nature. In reality, the fact that nobody has any brakes or gears, and that there are no corners, makes the track one of the safest places to race. The skills you develop will be an invaluable asset to you in all other aspects of your cycling.

Fixed gears used to be more or less standard in most forms of cycling. Many riders would use them for time trials and training all year round, but now they are usually used only on the track. If you have never ridden on a fixed-wheel bike, there is only one way to get used to it, and that is by going out and doing it! The effect of a fixed wheel is that you have to adopt a fast, supple and efficient pedalling action. You have no chance to change gear, which means that you will have to develop the ability to pedal quickly for long periods of time, without respite. To achieve this, you will need to concentrate on pedalling right through the revolution. Riding a fixed wheel on free rollers is an ideal way to develop a feel for it.

Your braking system, or rather slowing-down method, on a track bike is twofold. Easing back a little on the pedals will slow you slightly, just enough to miss a wheel or to open a gap. Riding up the banking, on the other hand, will cause you to slow down through the force of gravity.

Using the banking

The first time you peer up at 45-degree banking it is somewhat scary, to say the least, and you may well feel as if you

have been sent to face the wall of death. The principal rule is to relax and not to be scared of it: unless you do something exceptionally silly, or slow down to walking pace, it is harmless. Before you attempt to confront it in a

ABOVE: *Keeping a constant watch on the other riders is essential.*
LEFT: *In short events, timing and tactics have to be carefully calculated.*

....

bunch, spend some time on the track alone, riding round and round; at first you can just build up speed and work your way up the banking, then try swinging up and down it a few times.

The banking is there to help you: you can use it to control your pace, or to move backwards in a line-out. This is best done by going straight on as you come to the banking, then swinging down again. But always take a glance behind before doing this, to make sure

TRACK TIPS

1 Be constantly aware of your legs: whether you are moving quickly or slowly, never stop pedalling or ease up, or you will go over the bars.

2 Ride smoothly: never make erratic moves or come inside a rider unless there is plenty of room.

3 Whenever there is a lull in the pace, expect an attack to come on the banking: listen and look for shadows.

4 Learn the rules of track racing thoroughly before you compete. Know what is and is not permitted, but be aware of how the rules are interpreted in action: you may be able to push them to the limit.

5 Try to avoid getting boxed in near the finish, or when a lull occurs, by riding slightly to the outside of the rider in front.

6 Keeping watch over your shoulder is important, as it tells you when other riders are moving up.

The banking is used to manoeuvre yourself into the best position, as a natural brake and for making attacks. It looks daunting, but once you're used to it, it is a great help.
LEFT: *Bunched racing is a very close-contact sport, but is much safer than it looks.*

that no-one is coming up behind you.

The other prime use for the banking is a tactical one. The effect of riding at an angle down the banking is similar to riding downhill, in that it causes you to accelerate; this makes the banking a prime springboard for attacks. Such attacks are usually made by discreetly accelerating from behind, moving up the banking and then sprinting down into the next straight.

Riding in a bunch

Riding in a fast-moving track bunch can be extremely exhilarating, and is usually very safe, but if you do make a mistake the chances are you will find that every rider behind you is suddenly lying on top of you. This is why it is essential to practise riding on a track before racing. Many local tracks run sessions where you can try out track bikes and learn to ride safely.

The golden rule is that at all times you must be totally focused on what is going on around you. Use your ears to listen for movement behind, and your eyes to watch ahead. While staying relaxed, you must also be ready to react to any changes in pace or sudden attacks.

Never make any erratic movements which may be dangerous to other riders: when you get out of the saddle make sure that you do not throw your bike backwards, and always check behind before moving out of line.

Solo racing

Racing alone against the watch on the track is a supreme test of character and fitness. The races are so short that there is simply no room for error or misjudgement.

One of the shortest forms of solo race, the kilometre time trial, demands a great deal of explosive acceleration and power, but, at around one minute and ten seconds in duration for a top rider, very little stamina. Kilometre riders, therefore, tend to be solidly built power athletes who can keep an explosive effort going for that length of time. A fast start is paramount, and a fine judgement of pace is essential.

The perfect pursuit

The pursuit requires a great deal of speed, stamina and fitness, and a totally focused mind. It is in effect a short, and particularly intense, time trial. Good pursuiters tend also to be good road racers and time triallists.

A lightweight aerodynamic bike is essential if you intend to take pursuiting seriously. Equally, narrow, light tyres, aero wheels, tri-bars, a skin suit and an aero helmet all go towards saving those vital fractions of seconds that decide the outcome of a pursuit match.

You should select a gear that you can pedal at around 100rpm for the given distance. This varies from rider to rider: many pursuiters use gears of 50 x 15.

A good warm-up on a fixed trainer, at just below race level, is essential, as is a totally focused mind. It is very important that you are ready and do not feel rushed into the race.

It is vital to have a well-planned schedule for riding a pursuit. You should decide on this from a detailed analysis of your training tests, working out how fast you need to go and at what intensity you should be riding. It is very easy to overdo it too early in a pursuit, and a schedule will help you to avoid that. Having someone at the track to indicate to you whether you're up or down on your schedule is invaluable. Only once you get into the last 1,000 metres or so can you afford to go all out.

In such a short event, it is of paramount importance to have the right mental attitude, both in preparation and

TOP: *A rider leaves the starting blocks.*
LEFT: *Chris Boardman in full flight on his way to the world hour record at Manchester in 1996.*
RIGHT: *A schedule and on-track information during the race are vital for determining your output.*
FAR RIGHT:*To get everything out of your body during those vital minutes you must be fully prepared and completely committed.*

PURSUIT POINTS

1 Never panic and go over your limit if you see you are slightly behind. All riders have different paces.

2 Only ever do as much as you need to in a pursuit, as you will often have to ride two or three rounds.

3 Always keep mobile between matches. Also be aware that it can be a long time between rounds, so keep hydrated and nibble at an energy bar or similar source of carbohydrate.

4 Never start a race before you are totally ready and focused.

5 Make sure you know the event's rules, conditions and standards before you ride.

while racing. A pursuiter will have to develop a great deal of inner aggression to enable him or her to perform well within such a short period of time; this will involve visualising the race over and over again. Once the race is under way, it is necessary to focus 100 per cent on the task in hand. Forgetting the other rider, the pursuiter should concentrate on riding the distance as fast as possible, maintaining the schedule, constantly keeping up the power output, holding the blue pursuiters' line painted around the track, and riding smoothly. Any distraction from this will spoil the rhythm and cost time. Not until the closing stages should the progress of the other rider be noted.

Fitness

Fitness and health are worthy goals for all cyclists. They form the foundations on which every competitor relies. If you can build a consistent base of good health and fitness you will perform at your best, enjoy

your riding and have a rewarding cycling 'career'. Also spending a few hours a week on a bike is an injury-free means of increasing fitness and health and an effective way of relieving stress. But, although 'getting fit' is a worthwhile aim in itself, the racing cyclist tends to use fitness as a means to an end: as a

competitor, you will need to pay careful attention to your body's needs, including diet and specific event preparation.

A definition of fitness

Given the huge growth of the fitness industry over the past fifteen years, it is perhaps surprising that 'fitness' is seen by most people as a rather vague term. By looking carefully at how the body functions, we can see the relationship between fitness and health, and how cycling fits into the overall picture.

The term 'health' refers to freedom from illness and injury, whereas 'fitness' is the ability to do mechanical work (lifting or moving, for example) efficiently. Obviously, then, it is possible to be healthy without being fit, and vice versa. A cyclist, for example, may have developed a high degree of fitness through cycling and weight training, but may suffer from asthma, while another individual might be free from all signs or symptoms of illness, yet have a low level of fitness and tire easily when faced with physical tasks.

This is not to say that there is no link between health and fitness. Positive changes in fitness levels, achieved in a safe, controlled way, may help to prevent illness or disease, including certain serious medical conditions, of which the most common is heart disease. Exercise is both a means of reducing the risk of heart disease and an important part of rehabilitation for cardiac patients. This is due to the effects of exercise on many different but interrelated mechanisms in the body; these benefits may include reductions in blood pressure, body fat percentage and harmful cholesterol levels, and an improvement in the circulation around the whole body and the heart muscle itself.

Cycling is one of many ways in which you can improve the efficiency of your physiological systems, including the cardiovascular (heart and lungs), immune and nervous systems. The box on the right identifies some of the potential benefits of regular moderate exercise such as cycling.

To compare the body to a motor car, exercise improves efficiency in the fuel supply (the heart, lungs, circulation and energy stores), the ignition (the nervous system), the propulsion (muscle power), the exhaust system (circulation and lungs) and the chassis (bone, tendon and muscle structures). In addition, there is increasing evidence that moderate aerobic (cardiovascular) exercise improves immunity to illness. On the other hand, it is also true that the extreme forms of training undertaken by some serious racing cyclists may lead to short- or long-term suppression of the immune system.

The gains in health and fitness from regular exercise can be considerable, and may be measured after no more than a couple of weeks. As few as three 'brisk' rides per week,

The benefits of taking regular exercise

Health benefits of regular exercise
- Reduces the risk and severity of heart disease
- Prevents or reduces obesity
- Increases the metabolic rate (the number of calories used per day). This higher calorie use helps prevent obesity
- Reduces blood pressure in people who have existing high blood pressure
- Delays post-menopausal osteoporosis (a benefit less likely from cycling, a non-weight-bearing exercise)
- Improves glucose tolerance in diabetics
- Improves mental health and reduces stress levels

Fitness benefits of regular exercise
- Improves the oxygen delivery system (heart and lungs)
- Improves the blood supply to the muscles
- Improves the chemical processes in the muscles
- Helps to clear lactic acid from active muscles
- Increases the body's ability to use fats as fuel
- Strengthens muscles, tendons and ligaments
- Makes exercise effort appear easier
- Improves tolerance of heat, through increased sweating efficiency

(Adapted from Coronary Prevention Group report, Exercise, Heart, Health, London, 1987)

One of the ways in which an elite cyclist's fitness may be gauged is through a VO$_2$ Max test (the maximum amount of oxygen (in litres per minute) that the body can consume).

each lasting no more than 20 minutes, will have a beneficial effect on your cardiovascular system.

The components of fitness

Your ability to do mechanical work is related to how well you have developed the necessary 'components' of fitness. For example, moving a heavy weight many times requires two components: the initial strength to pick it up and endurance in the muscles being used.

The components of fitness can be divided into two groups: 'health-related' and 'sports-specific'. The health-related components are those which allow the body to function efficiently when performing everyday tasks. Of course, the majority of the population may score poorly on fitness tests and still function relatively well. However, good levels of health-related fitness make a person more able to cope with the physical demands of everyday life and less prone to many forms of illness.

Even people who already suffer from health problems may see improvement through a controlled exercise programme which is aimed at developing health-related fitness.

The components of health-related fitness are as follows:

- cardiovascular fitness: fitness of the lungs, heart and circulation;
- body composition: the ratio of fat to lean body tissue;
- flexibility: the range of movement in the joints, tendons and muscles;
- muscular strength: the force we can produce to move or lift;
- muscular endurance: the ability to do muscular work (moving or lifting) repeatedly.

Clearly, success in virtually any sport will require a high degree of the health-related components of fitness, and all-round conditioning will form the major part of an athlete's preparation. These components have a particularly crucial role in sports which involve relatively low skill

levels and continuous rhythmic movement, such as running and cycling.

There are also other factors which come into play in achieving sporting excellence, and in some sports, such as snooker, these will be of greater importance than the health-related components. These 'sports-related' fitness components are:

- speed: the ability to move rapidly;
- power: the ability to produce great forces very quickly;
- reaction time: the ability to react quickly to situations and events;
- skill: the ability to perform precise actions requiring co-ordination of the senses (sight, hearing, touch) with muscular movements;
- balance: required for many skills to be undertaken.

These elements combine the health-related components with a highly developed nervous system, which controls the sportsperson's ability to perform skilled movements and to produce high-speed muscle action. A soccer player, for example, will need good cardiovascular fitness in order to complete a 90-minute game, muscular strength and endurance for tackling, flexibility to help prevent injuries, speed and power to cover the ground rapidly and for jumping, and good reaction times, skill and balance for ball skills and to avoid challenges from the opposition.

Cycle-specific fitness

Bike racing in its various forms demands a high level of efficiency in many of the components of fitness, as described on pages 54–5.

As far as cycling is concerned, fitness is required to move the combined mass of the bicycle and rider against surface friction, air resistance and, when riding up an incline, the force of gravity. The watt is the unit of power which is most often used to measure cycling performance. Top riders are able to produce 400-450 watts for up to an hour, and over 1,000 watts in explosive efforts lasting ten seconds. Put simply, this means that an elite cyclist riding for an hour at maximum intensity is producing enough power to illuminate four to five 100-watt light bulbs for the whole hour! A recreational cyclist may achieve a sustained 150-200 watts, and 700-900 at peak power.

Cardiovascular conditioning

Assuming that you have enough force to get going in the first place, the physical factors that allow you to gain momentum and continue moving are your aerobic power and aerobic capacity. In simple terms, aerobic capacity is the amount of oxygen and fuel your blood can carry, together with the amount of oxygen, fuel and waste products your muscles can deal with, while aerobic power is the

ability to deliver fuel and oxygen rapidly to active muscle.

What this means in practice is that a cyclist needs to develop the systems that unload oxygen from the lungs, transport it in the blood, pump it from the heart through to the muscles, unload it at the muscles, burn fuel in the muscles and remove waste products from the whole system (e.g. lactic acid and carbon dioxide). Effective training can make all these functions more efficient, from the volume of blood pumped per heart beat to the number of blood capillaries that serve a group of muscle fibres and the efficiency of the nervous system as it fires the sparks that make it all happen.

The graph below shows heart rates

recorded during a moderate intensity ride. You can see the variations: due to hilly terrain some quite high heart rates were achieved solely in order to get over the steeper hills on the route. Doing a ride like this several times a week for ten to twelve weeks would be an excellent way to develop a foundation of cardiovascular conditioning, along with positive gains in muscular strength and endurance.

Racing fitness

When you look at the training sessions in the next chapter, you will see that they cover six aspects of fitness, each relating to a particular demand of racing (see above right). Each of these elements can be developed on its own or combined with others in an effective training plan. There are many overlaps and interrelationships between them, and you may have to use several or all of them during a race, or even simultaneously. For example, attacking (using explosive

•••••••••••••••••••••••••••••••••••••

Heart rates recorded during a recreational cycle ride.

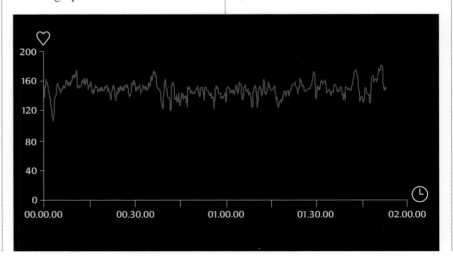

Muscle structure

Your ability to develop the various elements of fitness will be to some degree genetically determined. The nature of your muscle structure, in particular, affects both your performance and your response to training.

Muscles are made up of millions of fibres, arranged in bundles; these are supplied with fuel and oxygen by the circulation, while electrical stimulus to begin activity comes from the nervous system. There are three basic types of muscle fibre: slow oxidative (SO), fast oxidative glycolytic (FOG) and fast glycolytic (FG). The table below shows how they work.

For example, a successful track sprinter is likely to be genetically endowed with a high proportion of FG fibres in the propulsive muscles, a top road racer will have a balance of all three, with a tendency towards higher quantities of SO and FOG fibres, and a long-distance time triallist is most likely to have inherited a high percentage of SO fibres. The fibres can be trained to be more efficient (FOG being the most highly adaptable) and you may be able to slightly alter the type of fibres you have.

•••

THE SIX ELEMENTS OF FITNESS

1 **Aerobic capacity: the ability to ride for long periods of time at low levels of intensity.**

2 **Aerobic power: enables you to perform 'high-powered' endurance work lasting between three and eight minutes, such as in a 4,000-metre pursuit.**

3 **Intensity threshold: the highest level of intensity, in terms of heart rate, at which you can ride for sustained periods (over 20 minutes) without suffering rapid fatigue.**

4 **Muscular endurance: the ability to sustain repeated muscle contractions at a force higher than normally required, for example when powering over a short climb in a high gear.**

5 **Explosive power: the ability to develop near-maximal force in a very short time, as in a sprint effort.**

6 **Pain tolerance: the ability to continue a high work rate whilst suffering pain and discomfort in the propulsive muscles.**

•••

power) may be done whilst riding hard in a break (involving the intensity threshold), and you may then need to maintain a high speed (pain tolerance) as the finish line approaches. For further examples, see pages 58–9; training sessions designed to develop each of the various elements are included in Chapter 5.

The Lactic Acid threshold

What happens when you ride 'at the threshold' is that the rate of production of lactic acid (a by-product of high-intensity exercise relying on carbohydrates for fuel) is equal to the rate of its removal from the muscle. If you try to increase the power output, some lactic acid will build up in the muscle, the perception of effort will increase and fatigue will set in. You will then be forced to reduce your effort to restore the balance.

Effective training increases the power that can be produced before lactic acid begins to accumulate in the muscle. This is because it makes the energy pathways more efficient by better buffering of the lactic acid and increasing the ability of the blood to counteract the effects of high acidity.

Muscle type	Characteristics	Type of activity	Uses
slow oxidative	resistance to fatigue, using fat and carbohydrate as fuel	sustained low-resistance	aerobic capacity, aerobic power, intensity threshold
fast oxidative glycolytic	more reliant on carbohydrate as fuel, quite resistant to fatigue	faster, more intense	aerobic power, intensity threshold, muscle endurance
fast glycolytic	relies on carbohydrate and high-energy phosphates as fuel, rapid onset of fatigue	high-power	explosive power, pain tolerance

The various disciplines

When we look at the physical demands of the various branches of cycle racing, it becomes clear that for all but some specific track events, cardiovascular conditioning (aerobic capacity and power) is the essential bedrock on which success is built.

The ability to sustain aerobic exercise is most commonly referred to as endurance or aerobic fitness. Although it may seem surprising, the fact is that not only 24-hour time trials and 100-mile (160km) road races are endurance events: the 4,000-metre pursuit on the track is an endurance event, even though it may last for little more than four minutes.

If you have developed a high level of endurance fitness, you will be able to finish almost any form of cycle race. However, there is more to real success than this: you need to develop the specific fitness that will allow you to be a competitor rather than simply a participant.

Road racing

Unlike similar endurance sports, such as marathon running, in which the competitor aims for a 'steady state', road racing involves a variety of intensities. In terms of power output, an individual road race might require three hours at 200 watts, repeated three- to four-minute efforts of 500 watts and a maximal sprint of 1,500 watts at the end. This makes road racing extremely demanding for the

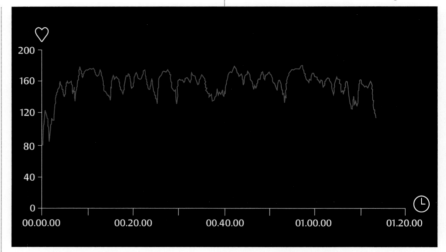

rider, and means that all aspects of fitness must be covered in training.

The only way to achieve regular success in road races is to be able to

deal with the many variables that the event can throw at you. Because road racing is so tactical, and there are so many possible race-winning strategies, you must be a jack of all fitness trades – and a master of quite a few, as well. A road racer should start with a high degree of aerobic fitness, in terms of both capacity and power, then add muscular endurance and the ability to tolerate pain in the muscles. You will need to be able to make, or respond to,

repeated attacks, using explosive power, and to ride at your intensity threshold (see page 57). Finally, your body must have the capacity to burn fat as fuel and to conserve carbohydrate stores for use later in an event.

The graph on page 58 shows the variation in intensity during the first four laps of an eight-lap, 75-mile (120km) road race. The heart rate ranges from lows of 130 to highs above 180. Even greater extremes may be experienced during a stage race, where a competitor may ride at below 100 beats per minute while in the centre of a large peloton on a

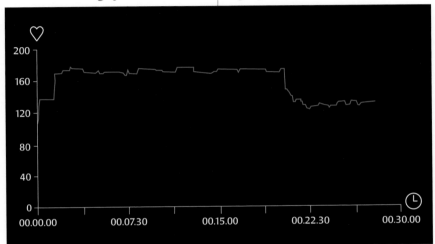

ABOVE LEFT: *A rider's heart rate recorded during four laps of a road race.*
ABOVE: *A rider's heart rate recorded during a ten-mile (16km) time trial.*
LEFT: *Steady-state riding using a HRM will provide a foundation of conditioning.*

••••••••••••••••••••••••••••••••

quiet day, then at near-maximal levels during attacks and counter-attacks.

Generally, the importance of aerobic capacity and power increases in proportion to the length of the event, with the shorter events, such as criteriums, demanding greater explosive power and pain tolerance. However, there is no escaping the fact that the successful road racer must possess high levels of all the elements of fitness: aerobic capacity as an

endurance base, aerobic power for more intense sustained efforts, such as short climbs, the ability to ride near to the intensity threshold for time-trial stages and lone breakaways, explosive power for effective sprints and attacks, and pain tolerance for occasional forays over the intensity threshold. Muscular endurance needs to be developed for riding into headwinds and for short climbs when high speeds must be maintained.

Time trialling

As a time triallist, you must have the ability to bring your heart rate rapidly up to your 'threshold' level, then to maintain this level for the duration of the event. The threshold will vary depending on the length of the test, with sustainable heart rates for ten-mile (16km) events being up to fifteen beats higher than for 50 miles (80km). You may also need to work on some specific fitness areas, depending on the distance to be ridden: for example, pain tolerance and a high aerobic capacity are needed for longer events. Attributes such as explosive power are less essential for riding time trials.

The graph below shows heart-rate readings for a ten-mile (16km) time trial. As you can see, the rider quickly raises her heart rate to a threshold level of 165-170 and maintains it there, with occasional fluctuations caused by inclines and descents.

Track racing

As a whole, track racing covers such a variety of disciplines that all elements of fitness are required, although track riders who specialise in certain types of event will need to concentrate on the appropriate areas. A sprinter, for example, can work on explosive power alone, whereas a points race rider must train to develop the whole range of fitness.

The one factor that distinguishes the track from other disciplines is the need to develop a high cadence or pedalling speed. This is produced by changes in the electrical impulses from the nervous system to the muscles, and can be achieved only by many hours of high-cadence riding. If you spend a great deal of time racing on the track at high pedalling speeds, you will find that you lose a certain amount of power and strength for other disciplines, such as road racing. This is because high-cadence riding, with a relatively low pedal resistance, tends to develop the endurance-related slow oxidative (SO) muscle fibres (see page 57), creating a corresponding decline in the efficiency of the strength-oriented fast glycolytic (FG) fibres, while the fast oxidative glycolytic (FOG) fibres become more adapted to the demands of endurance work.

Nutrition

It often seems that cyclists have an unusually close relationship with food. Indeed, many proclaim that the best thing about cycling is that it allows them to eat more than normal without gaining weight! However, if you take the right approach to what and how much you eat, you should see dramatic improvements in your performance.

U nfortunately, many of us love foods which in terms of performance – and sometimes health – do more harm than good. So much misinformation surrounds the subject of food and diet in relation to sport that it is very easy to be confused, especially by the claims of miracle 'performance foods'.

The nutrients which we gain from food perform several functions: carbohydrates give energy, proteins are largely responsible for building and repairing tissue, and vitamins and minerals help regulate the body's functions. For this reason, your diet must be suitably varied to provide all the nutrients you need for both normal living and sports training. It is not enough to eat a small selection of foods which you know are healthy, and nothing else; you need a variety of nutritious foods. Baked potatoes, for instance, are a good source of energy, but eating nothing but baked potatoes would not provide all the necessary vitamins, minerals, fats and proteins. Like a well-tuned racing car, the well-trained cyclist needs to put the best fuel into his or her body, together with the other nutrients,

such as iron, that are essential for efficient operation. Obviously, if you are training regularly, you will need to take in more calories than an inactive person, but most of these should be in the form of carbohydrates (e.g. 55-70 percent calories).

The sample meals on the right are intended to give you some idea of the types and quantities of food required by a cyclist in training. This is not a diet to be followed rigidly, and may not give the total calorie intake that you need.

Carbohydrates

For endurance athletes such as cyclists, one of the most important parts of the diet is the intake of carbohydrates. The body can use either carbohydrates, fat or protein as sources of fuel, but it prefers carbohydrates for very high-intensity exercise, such as the crucial moments of competition. So it is a good idea to ensure that you have an adequate store of carbohydrates in your body, and to maintain your intake of them during long training rides and races (see also pages 62–3). 'Complex'

carbohydrates are of greatest benefit; these are found in pasta, rice, bread, grains, potatoes and other similar foods. Try always to choose the whole-grain varieties of rice, pasta or bread. Such foods should make up around 60 per cent of your total calories.

Other foods to attack with relish are fresh fruits and vegetables, legumes (peas, beans), oily fish (see below) and chicken. Generally, aim to eat food that is as fresh and free of additives, colours and GM ingredients as is possible.

BREAKFAST
75g bran cereal with 500ml skimmed milk or soya milk
1 banana
1 slice wholemeal bread with
1 teaspoon olive oil margarine
250ml fruit juice

LUNCH
150g lean meat
1 wholemeal bread roll
2 teaspoons mayonnaise or mustard
3 tablespoons coleslaw
Lettuce and tomato
2 oatmeal biscuits
1 fresh peach
500ml water

DINNER
Chicken stir-fry (75g chicken, 250g diced vegetables, 2 teaspoons olive oil)
150g wholegrain rice
200g orange and grapefruit segments
275ml live yoghurt
500ml fruit juice

SNACK
150g microwave popcorn
500ml fruit juice

Fat

The most overlooked and most misunderstood component of the cyclist's diet is fat. Many people avoid it like the plague, yet in the correct foods it provides both energy and vital nutrients. Fats are an essential source of vitamin E, which is a powerful anti-oxidant, breaking down the toxins which result from high-intensity exercise. Athletes who try to cut out fat completely are likely to damage their health as well as their performance. What is required is a balanced approach to fat in the diet, with moderate consumption of healthy fats (e.g 20-25% of calories) and minimal harmful fats (e.g. saturated and hydrogenated fats). The good fats are found in oily fish (mackerel, sardines, herring), extra-virgin olive oil and some supplements, such as evening primrose oil and flax oil.

Dietary supplements

It has been said that the most nutritious substance in the world is the sewage from an Olympic village! This implies that athletes are relying too heavily on unnecessary vitamin, mineral and other supplements, which are merely expelled by the body.

Scientists have not yet come to a conclusion as to whether supplements are of benefit to sportspeople. On the one hand, it is argued that cyclists who are racing and training hard need more vitamins than a sedentary person. On the other hand, they tend to eat more food, and so will absorb more essential nutrients through their normal diet. Given the fact that modern production methods may affect the amount and quality of nutrients present in food, and

that many cyclists' diets are probably far from perfect, it may be wise to take a high-quality multi-vitamin and mineral supplement as a 'safety net', just in case your diet is not providing all you need.

Fluid intake and replacement

Although many riders are not aware of it, proper fluid replacement before, during and after racing will produce a clear improvement in performance. Maintaining body fluid levels during training and competition is especially important in hot weather, when the amount of water lost from the body through the skin and expired air can be over one litre per hour.

It is not a good idea to judge your fluid needs after exercising in hot weather by whether or not you feel thirsty, partly because drinking quickly dulls the thirst sensation. Another important point is that plain water dilutes the blood rapidly and causes an increase in urine production, leading to greater dehydration. Drinks containing some sodium (salt) – the major

electrolyte lost in sweat – will help you rehydrate more rapidly, because they maintain thirst and delay urine production. Your rehydration drink should also contain 6–8 per cent glucose or sucrose (see pages 62–3), as these carbohydrates provide a source of energy for working muscles, stimulate the gut to absorb fluid and improve the taste.

REHYDRATION GUIDELINES

1 Drink 500ml of rehydration fluid two hours before starting training or competition.

2 Drink 250ml of fluid fifteen minutes before the event.

3 Drink at least 150ml of carbohydrate sports drink every fifteen to twenty minutes during training and competition.

4 Do not restrict your fluid intake before or during an event.

5 Weigh yourself without clothes before and after training and racing, especially during hot weather. For each kilogram of body weight lost, drink one and a half litres of rehydration fluid.

6 Use a rehydration drink containing sodium to replenish lost body fluids quickly. The drink should also contain glucose or sucrose.

7 Avoid drinking alcohol because it stimulates urine production and increases dehydration.

Eating for competition

Despite a huge number of myths surrounding race nutrition, your diet before and during competition should be very similar to your normal training intake, and based on the same principles. Above all, it is important that you start a race with your body's carbohydrate stores completely replenished, and that you are fully hydrated.

The build-up to competition normally involves a reduction in the total training load (see pages 84–5), so in effect your total calorie requirements are reduced. However, you must ensure 60-70 percent your calories are derived from carbohydrates, and that you are taking sufficient water on board to eliminate the threat of dehydration. This is crucial, as carbohydrate is stored in the muscles with water; a high carbohydrate intake with low fluid intake can lead to water being drawn from other tissues, leaving you close to dehydration before the event starts.

Carbohydrate intake

It is important to consume the correct amount of carbohydrate before, during and after any event lasting an hour or more (or repeated efforts such as you might make during an interval session). Below are some

simple equations which will help you calculate what is most effective for you.

Your pre-race meal should be taken three hours before the event, so that you start with an empty stomach. To help you work out how much of what foods you will need, the box (right)

CARBOHYDRATE INTAKE

1 Weigh yourself (in kilograms). Call this figure W

2 Total carbohydrate intake (in grams) on the day before competition: W x 8

3 Carbohydrate intake (grams) in your pre-event meal: W x 3

4 Hourly carbohydrate consumption during training and event (grams): W x 0.7 to W x 1.25

5 Immediate post-race carbohydrate intake (grams): W to W x 1.5 plus protein intake (grams): W x 0.4

6.Carbohydrate content in next meal after the event: W x 1.0 to W x 1.5

contains a list of food portions which give you 50 grams of carbohydrate.

Energy drinks

These mysterious fluids are often baffling: do you need them or not, and will they propel you to victory? Your body's carbohydrate stores (called glycogen) are good for about

Energy drinks must be mixed to the recommended condentrations, otherwise they will not work properly.

90 minutes of hard riding or an hour if high intensity intervals are included. Once the glycogen is used up, your body becomes reliant on carbs circulating in your blood stream (i.e. from foods and drinks you eat earlier). So if you can consume some sports drinks or high carb foods as you ride, the problem is partially solved. Eating solid foods can be an adequate form of energy intake in many race situations, but energy drinks provide complex carbohydrates (the ones that

make pasta such a good energy food) in a bottle. You can replace some of the energy that you lose as you ride, without the practical difficulties of eating solid food while cycling.

That is the theory behind energy drinks. However, the various kinds of energy drink are as different as a plate of pasta and a chocolate bar; while both chocolate and pasta contain sugar, the pasta contains the type of complex sugar that is better for stomach comfort and race performance. Although simple sugars will provide the required energy, there are two potential flaws with them. Firstly, drinking them before you exercise can in fact lead to a fall in the levels of blood sugar available for fuel; secondly, they can be too sweet to drink comfortably when mixed at the necessary concentrations. Look at the labels on different makes of energy drink, and choose one that contains what are known as glucose polymers (also called maltodextrin, long-chain glucose or complex carbohydrates). In addition to polymers, some also contain ingredients such as fructose, electrolytes and vitamins.

Once you have selected a suitable product, try it out in training, as stomach cramps can occur when you use a drink unsuitable for your stomach. Aim to drink a 400ml (winter) to 750ml (summer) per hour; your stomach can take this amount easily, but it can be hard to remember simply to put the bottle to your mouth when racing at high intensities.

A final note on the use of energy drinks: reports have started to emerge of dental problems resulting from frequent use of carbohydrate drinks. If

you use them every day in training, you should aim to brush your teeth thoroughly before and afterwards.

Energy gels

An alternative source of energy for training and competition, energy gels have come onto the market fairly recently. These have similar ingredients

Bidons prepared with race food and ready to be handed to riders.

to energy drinks, but are concentrated and viscous and usually sold in a small sachet. Whilst they provide an excellent means of carrying carbohydrate supplements on the bike, they should be used only in conjunction with additional water intake; otherwise, they can cause dehydration, as water is drawn from other tissues to help in the digestion of the gel. That aside, they have a definite role to play in increasing the performance of endurance cyclists; in particular, they enable riders to carry water for drinking, which many prefer to flavoured commercial drinks.

Stretching and massage

When you are training hard, both your health and your fitness depend on how well you are able to recover. Fortunately, stretching and massage, two highly effective means of helping you to adapt to the rigours of cycling, are cheap and readily available.

For many cyclists, the term stretching seems to conjure up an image of some form of torture, and the deliberate stretching of muscles comes far down on their list of training priorities. However, in addition to aiding faster recovery and lessening your chances of injury, stretching can also help you to produce more power from your muscles.

One of the results of hard riding is a gradual loss of muscle elasticity and an overall reduction in joint flexibility. Since stretching improves flexibility and increases the range of motion, well-exercised muscles and joints will suffer less severe stress in race conditions. In turn, the longer your muscles and joints can perform under stress without failure, the longer you can cycle at speed. The stiffness and tightness that are frequently felt after a ride can be brought under control, and even eliminated, with proper stretching after you have completed a training session or race.

One of the best ways to achieve this is static stretching, in which you stretch each muscle slowly and carefully until a mild amount of tightness (not pain) is felt. The most important muscle groups for cyclists to work on in stretching sessions are the calves, the quadriceps (front of the thigh), the hamstring (back of the thigh), the back and the shoulder area.

Always begin with a very gentle stretch, maintaining the position for about 20 seconds, or until the muscle begins to relax. As you hold the stretch, the feeling of tension should diminish. If it does not, just ease off slightly until you are more comfortable. After holding the easy stretch, extend it by a fraction of an inch until you feel mild tension again. This position should be held for another 5–30 seconds. Again, the feeling of tension should reduce slightly or stay the same. If it increases, or the muscle becomes painful, you are over-stretching: ease off a bit to a comfortable stretch. Repeating this process a few times for each muscle group will give the best results.

You should never 'bounce' when stretching, as you may cause tiny tears in the muscle, leaving scar tissue behind; this can make the muscles less flexible than they were before.

Stretching is not something you should do only as part of a workout. If the timing of your workout does not allow for stretching – for example if you have to squeeze your training into a lunch break – then any other time of the day is fine. A routine of two to five minutes of stretching, several times a day, is excellent for keeping the muscles fine-tuned and tension-free. For more specific instructions, consult a fitness specialist at a gym or health club, or read one of the many specialist publications available on stretching for sport.

Massage

The principal aims of massage are to stimulate blood flow through the muscles, to drain the toxic by-products of exercise away from the muscles through the lymphatic system, and to re-align tangled or knotted muscle fibres. Because massage is always done towards the heart, it imitates the pumping action of active muscles through one-way valves in the veins, known as 'venous return'.

Four basic actions are used in massage. Stroking is done with the palm of the hand and the fingers, covering large ares with each sweep. The stroking can be light, increasing the blood flow to the skin, or deep, using moderate pressure from the heel of the hand. This is probably the most appropriate form of massage to perform on yourself if you are inexperienced.

Kneading is a more powerful movement, in which the hands grab, lift, squeeze and roll the muscle, working along its length. Friction massage involves small movements over a limited area, usually with the

MASSAGE HINTS

1 **You do not need a special table: use a towel on the kitchen table or on the carpet.**
2 **Use body oil or lotion to aid smooth rubbing.**
3 **Rub towards the heart; glide back to start each stroke.**
4 **Never massage over injuries; this is for experienced injury masseurs only.**
5 **Keep areas not being massaged warm with towels or clothing.**
6 **When you are massaging yourself, prop your foot on a chair with the knee bent to reach the calf and the back of the thigh without straining your back.**
7 **If you like the idea of regular massage, a local cycling club may have details of experienced sports masseurs in your area.**

tips of the fingers or thumbs; the pressure is moderate to high. It is most often used on the sites of injuries or painful muscle spasms. Percussion is the 'slapping' massage sometimes shown in films. This is most often done by inexperienced masseurs who want to look as if they are working hard, and seldom occurs in serious sports massage.

It is worth trying massage out, even if it is just the cheap, do-it-yourself version. If nothing else, it will help you to relax after training, as long as you are very careful not to dig too deeply into sore muscles. If you have always wondered why many riders shave their legs, one massage will answer the question; the rubbing goes against the direction of hair growth and is pretty painful without smooth legs and lubrication.

Start with the front of the thigh, using the thumb and fingers to massage each muscle gently. The circulation through the knee can be stimulated using the thumbs in a circular motion; avoid pressing too hard on the joint.

Move onto the shin, stroking the muscles on either side of the shin bone upwards towards the knee. Cross-rubbing (or 'roffing' as it is known) over the calf muscles helps to loosen the muscle before the stroking actions later in the massage.

Next rub gently up the back of the thigh, from the knee to the hip. Try a 'kneading' action, followed by stroking.

Working on the back of the calves again, use the fingers to smooth out the muscle, and stroke the palm of the hands up its full length. Gentle 'kneading' by the thumb and forefinger on the Achilles tendon increases the blood flow through it, which is usually much lower than the blood flow through muscle.

Finish off with flushing strokes along the full length of the legs: first the back, then the front.

The cyclist's neck is often under stress when riding, particularly with the hands on the 'drops'. A simple kneading action on the muscles at the back of the neck and top of the shoulders can ease any discomfort and aid relaxation. Firm pressure with the thumbs on the upper neck will dispel headaches caused by the stress of racing.

Massage may be used for relaxation and recovery, or, in the hands of an experienced masseur, for the treatment of injuries.

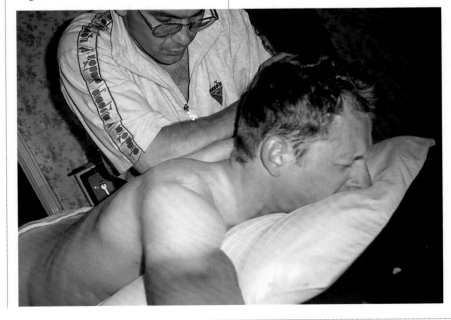

Total body conditioning

Apart from being supple and well warmed up before riding, one of the best means of ensuring that you stay injury-free is through working on muscles that cycling fails to develop; this is known as total body conditioning, and is vital in all athletically demanding sports.

For cyclists, total body conditioning includes upper and lower body training. Whilst the main aim is to avoid injury, it is likely that a more even muscular development may also improve cycling performance. More efficient muscles require less energy to keep you in an upright position on your bike. This liberates blood flow and fuel supplies for the propulsive muscles. In addition, well-conditioned muscles are efficient at combatting lactic acid build-up during racing and training. There is some evidence that during intense exercise, while the legs are producing lactic acid in high concentrations, relaxed and well-conditioned upper-body muscles can convert the lactic acid into fuel to be sent back to the muscle cells of the legs.

The following plan has been put together for riders who are seeking all-round muscular conditioning. If you do not have access to weight-training facilities, you can buy second hand equipment at very reasonable prices and therefore not have to travel to a gym each time you want to weight train.

Each session should involve two to four sets of eight to twelve repetitions of each of the exercises. Fatigue should stop you doing more than twelve repetitions in each set. To

SHOULDER PRESS Hold a weight in each hand by your sides; raise your hands to shoulder level, then push them above your head, straightening your arms to vertical. Stop just before your arms are straight, and slowly return them to the starting position.

SQUAT Place your feet shoulder width apart with a weight in either hand or resting on your shoulders. Slowly squat towards the floor keeping your back straight and bending at the knee. Lower until your knees are at right angles, hold for a count of two then slowly return to the starting position.

BICEPS CURL Start with your arms by your sides, holding a weight in each hand. Keeping your palms facing away from you and your elbows at your waist, slowly raise your hands to your chest. Then return to the starting position.

LEG EXTENSION (machine - shown below) Sit with a straight back and the pad resting on your ankles. Slowly raise the bar by straightening your legs, until they are fully extended. Hold for a count of two then lower back down. Return the legs to just ahead of vertical rather than all the way back to the machines original starting position.

BENT ROW Stand with a weight in either hand or a bar in both hands hanging at the thighs. Slowly bend at the waist until your flat back is almost parallel to the floor. Pull the weight upwards towards the chest until the elbows are at a right angle. Hold at this point for a count of three then slowly lower the weight to the starting posititon.

LAT RAISE Hold a weight in each hand by your sides, then raise your arms to the side until your hands are level with your shoulders. Slowly return to the starting position.

HAMSTRING CURL Lie face down on the machine with the pad resting on the Achilles. Ensure you are not over extending your back. Next, slowly bend the knee raising the weight upwards until your foot is almost on your bottom. Hold for a count of two then very slowly lower the weight to the starting position. Be sure not to do this exercise too fast as the hamstrings can be easily injured.

ABDOMINAL CURL Lying on your back, bend your knees up and place your feet flat on the floor. Put your hands on your thighs and slowly slide them up to your knees by curling up your shoulders and head. Hold for a count of two then return slowly to the starting position.

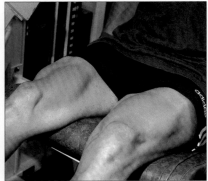

If winter weather is so bad that it makes normal training actually unpleasant, or even unsafe, both the upper and lower body can be kept in condition, either at home or in a gym.

start with, you will need to experiment to find the resistance required for each exercise; the idea is that you should only just be able to complete the last repetition in each set. For the abdominal curl, the last set should continue until you are unable to do the exercise correctly.

Winter is the ideal time to begin these exercises, and for best effects you should carry out a weight-training session two or at most three times a week. Once you have built up your upper-body muscle, just one session a week either at home or in the gym will be enough to maintain it through the season.

Your personal training programme

Many riders base their training on what amounts to nothing other than trial and error. This is far from ideal, as it depends on stumbling across the correct training

method by chance. In simple terms, training involves subjecting your body to physical stress, forcing it to adapt so that it will be able to cope more easily with a similar level of stress in the future. If you make the stress specific to the demands of competition, the resulting adaptations will enable you to perform at a higher level. This chapter shows you

how training works in principle, and then goes on to guide you through the process of preparing a training plan tailored to your own racing needs.

The principles of training

Training for improved cycling performance is governed by certain laws or principles. If you understand these and take them fully into account, you will make the best use of your training time and effort.

When you first begin training, your body goes through a 'shock' period – a day of pain following your first weight-training session, for example. This soon wears off, and you start to see significant gains: it is quite common for beginners to take huge chunks out of their time for a particular ride.

In time, however, you will find that the rate of progression slows, and after a few years of dedicated training it is not abnormal to reach a 'plateau' in fitness – or even to go downhill.

In order to get off the plateau, or to reverse a decline in condition, most riders increase either the amount or the intensity of their training. The cyclist's traditional approach has always been that the more miles you ride the fitter you will be, and yet taken to extremes this will result in a breakdown of the immune system and muscle tissues – chronic overtraining.

When you are planning a training programme, you must take into account several rules or principles if you are to achieve the desired results and avoid hitting a 'plateau'. These are listed below and on pages 72–3. Ignoring any of them, or applying them only partially, will prevent you from making the most of your valuable training time.

The overcompensation principle

The crucial idea behind all training is this: the only way to improve your fitness is by stressing the body – or a particular system or structure in the body – and then allowing it to recover from that stress. To put this another way, the body adapts in order to survive changes in its environment: for example, continuous exposure to high altitude (a physical stress) leads to alterations in the blood chemistry. By deliberately and systematically subjecting yourself to such stresses, it is possible to achieve adaptations in whatever physiological system you wish to improve. If you are keen to gain strength in your arm muscles, you could try lifting large weights; riding at an intensity at which fats are the body's main fuel will increase the efficiency of its fat-burning systems.

The diagram below illustrates this principle. After a training session or series of sessions, your body experiences fatigue. As it recovers, it adapts to the stress and is in a better biological condition than before. This series of reactions to training stress is known as overcompensation. However, the improvements last for only a limited period: if the body is left to its own devices, it will return to its previous condition.

The overload principle

This idea, which is related to the overcompensation principle, works on the basis that in order to improve your strength, muscle size or endurance through training you must exercise against a resistance greater than that 'normally' encountered. If you ride

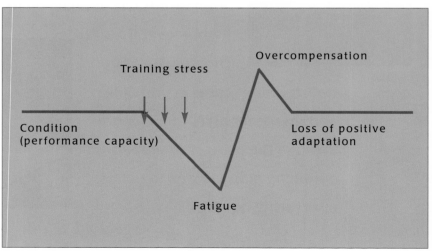

How the overcompensation principle works in relation to training.

for the same distance and at the same speed during every workout, there will be no continued improvement beyond the point to which your body has already adapted. Many riders fail to stress their body sufficiently, and as a consequence their race results never improve. If your training routine has not changed a great deal for the past few years – the same weekly routine, the same routes, the same speed – you need to introduce some overload into the equation.

Training overload has three components, which are vital when you are planning your training sessions. Briefly, they are as follows:

- intensity of training: how hard you are training, measured by heart rate, speed and perception of effort;
- duration of training: how long you are spending at a given intensity, either continuously or in repeated efforts during a ride;
- frequency of training.

A potential problem with the need for overload is that the body is wonderfully adaptable to stresses imposed during training. This can mean that the stress levels required for continued improvement become so great that your powers of recovery simply cannot keep up. You can overcome this by redesigning your training to target areas in which you are weak, or to train one system or structure while another is recovering (see pages 72–3).

The specificity principle

Back to the 'plateau' now. Say you have been training and racing for years, and now you find that your results are getting no better or even slightly worse. What should you do? The answer is to look at the demands of the events you are riding and the specific physical attributes necessary to succeed. Then examine your training in relation to these attributes.

For example, if you need to be able to ride at 28 miles an hour for success in time trials, think about how much time you spend training at this kind of intensity. You cannot expect to do something in a race that you never do in training! Similarly, consider the average three-hour road race. Within the field, most if not all riders are capable of covering the distance. However, road races are not won on endurance fitness alone: successful riders need to have the specific fitness to react to attacks within the race, or to make winning moves. They need explosive power, strength, speed and an ability to suffer – attributes that the typical rider's long miles of training will not develop. Very few cyclists train for anything other than to be fitter, but this is different from training to compete successfully. In reality, the 'traditional' approach of most riders means wasting hours doing hundreds of miles and yet never approaching race intensity.

The key point behind the overcompensation principle is that muscles which are stressed during cycle training and racing will adapt to the specific demands you impose upon them, as will body systems and tissues other than your muscles. For this reason, your training should be designed to bring about improvements in the areas of fitness necessary for the event in which you wish to be successful. (Note that the point here is not that the best training for racing is racing, though competition can have a beneficial effect.)

This is where the six elements of fitness described on pages 56–7 come in. If your training objectives include becoming a more explosive sprinter, then you have to train using explosive power. If you need greater endurance, you must include aerobic capacity rides in your programme. The key is knowing what you are training for.

The specificity principle is so uncompromising in its workings that problems frequently arise if a rider is trying to make improvements in more than one element of fitness at a time. The specific training required for one area may well reduce the progress you can expect to make in another. For example, training for aerobic power will severely limit the level of strength you can attain.

Summary

To sum up, your training needs to borrow from both the traditional 'miles' approach and more modern training methods based on the elements of fitness. Distance rides can be used to gain a base of conditioning to complete events, while the specificity principle is applied to develop the higher-end fitness to *compete* in events. The first part is easy, and is in fact what most riders do all the time. The second needs some thought and requires a specific plan – not just going out and riding your bike.

Avoiding overtraining

Although knowing when and how to train is vital if you are to achieve success in your chosen sport, it is also important that you know when not to train. Experienced cyclists, especially professionals, whose bodies are in peak condition, know that rest is one of the key factors affecting performance.

*I*t is an unfortunate fact that the principles of training also work in reverse: if you stop stressing your body, it will adapt to meet the reduced stress. In other words, when you stop your training programme you will not keep your hard-won fitness gains forever. Even more unfortunately, it takes far less time to become 'de-trained' than it does to become trained.

The good news, however, is that after you have developed a high level of fitness through a foundation of hard training, the same amount of work is not necessary to maintain peak performance levels. The frequency of hard training sessions can be reduced by at least a half and yet your condition will remain close to 100 per cent. So if you know that you need to do fifteen hours of training a week to achieve a base of endurance fitness, seven hours a week at the same intensity will maintain it.

As well as being very useful for the inevitable periods when other commitments mean you are too busy to train as frequently as usual, this reduction in the number of hard training sessions required will allow you to make better use of your training time. Instead of doing nothing

but long miles, you will be able to develop the specific attributes needed for your branch of racing, while maintaining your fitness base.

Rest and recovery

Another way of describing the processes that occur during training is known as the 'general adaptation

syndrome'. This consists of three stages: the 'alarm stage', caused by the application of training stress (the overload principle), the 'resistance stage', when your muscles and other systems adapt in order to resist the stressful training more efficiently (the overcompensation principle), and the 'exhaustion stage', where, if you persist in applying stress, you will exhaust your 'reserves' and then be forced to stop training through the sheer collapse of the physiological systems involved.

You can get away with continual hard training for only so long: in time, your body will say 'no', and your performance, and often your health,

LEFT: *Racing is both physically and mentally draining, so you need to make sure that you look after yourself before and after the event.* ABOVE: *Over-training can be at the root of poor performances that have no other apparent cause.*

will suffer. One way of overcoming this is by planning your training in cycles, where three weeks of build-up are followed by a 'recovery' week of low-intensity training or complete rest in order to facilitate overcompensation. You can then begin the next cycle with an increased training load. If you train before overcompensation has occurred, the result will be a steady decline in your physical state, requiring a longer rest and recovery period. Using 'active' rest periods in the training plan

is a technique that has been used for decades by other endurance athletes, especially swimmers, but it has tended to be dismissed without consideration by many cycling coaches.

Rest and recuperation allow your body to repair microscopic damage to muscles and to restore energy levels, both of which are necessary if you are

going to race successfully. All too often, a rider will experience a few poor results and try to train harder, when practically always it is rest that is required. Recent studies on elite endurance athletes have shown marked improvements in performance following up to two weeks of rest.

However, you should not see recuperation as nothing more than lying on the sofa with your feet up. Whilst there is much truth in the cyclist's adage of 'never stand when you can sit and never sit when you can lie', there are many ways of actively restoring the body to a fully conditioned state. Massage is an essential part of a professional cyclist's life, yet few amateurs realise that it

can help them, too. (See pages 64–5 for more details.)

Other useful recovery techniques include using a cold shower on your legs, taking aspirin (or a similar anti-inflammatory) to alleviate muscle pain, stretching, elevating the legs, and of course a well planned diet with adequate sleep (>7h per night).

Many top racers who are training hard have an afternoon siesta: it is surprising how refreshing thirty minutes' sleep can be. Riders who have to fit their training into the real world of full-time work could try taking a nap on the train or bus or at the weekend.

Know your body

One of the keys to successful racing is an intimate knowledge of your body, enabling you to predict how it will react to the various demands that you are likely to make on it during training and racing. This is something that may take a few years to develop. Learn to sense the condition of your muscles, how much sleep you need and whether your diet is good enough. In particular, look out for signs of overtraining: insomnia, loss of appetite, loss of enthusiasm, irritability and so on. You should be able to tell if a hard ride is possible by the feeling in your legs soon after you get up in the morning.

Learning what your body is saying is one thing; doing what it says is another. If you feel terrible, why train at all? If you feel great, replace the easy ride you had planned with a hard interval-training session. In short, do not be a slave to your training plan: learn to be flexible.

Training aids

Although getting on your bike and riding as much as you can may seem the only way to get fitter, there are several devices which can make your training more productive.

You will probably come across a great deal of merchandise which the manufacturers claim will make you a better rider. However, there are only three aids which are essential to the cyclist in serious training: a heart-rate monitor (HRM), a cycle computer and a 'turbo' or 'indoor' trainer. The cycle computer is covered in more detail on pages 128–9: suffice it to say here that it can be invaluable for monitoring your progress.

Stationary trainers

The turbo trainer, 'rollers' or indoor trainer is a device with many uses: to allow you to train indoors for endurance (often essential in the winter months), to enable fitness testing, for quality sessions and to allow pre-race warming up. Normally, the front of the bike is clamped into a frame and the rear wheel turns on rollers. Simple models rely on fans to provide resistance as they spin through the air, while more complex types include heart-rate monitoring, programmable changes in resistance and fitness-testing features.

A stationary trainer is best used on a solid floor, as suspended floors can cause uncomfortable vibrations to travel through the bike frame. Make sure the room is well ventilated, and if possible use an electric fan to minimise body temperature increases. If you overheat, the heart rates you achieve will be as a result of your body trying to cool down, so you will not be training at the right intensity. Keep sessions relatively short – 45 minutes to an hour – and have a drink close at hand to avoid dehydration.

Be aware that using a stationary trainer may place additional stress on the bike frame and may also cause some cyclists to develop knee problems. Because the frame is so rigidly locked into the trainer, the joints have less freedom to move than normal, and can therefore become painful and swollen. New types of trainer, incorporating a suspension mounting, should avoid any such problems, which can become serious.

If your bike has a rear-wheel-mounted computer, or your trainer measures speed or power in watts, you can monitor your fitness level. Before doing the test, you need to calibrate the trainer to ensure that you get reliable results. Pedal until you reach a set speed or power output, then stop and time how long it takes for your rear wheel to stop turning. Each time you run the test, adjust the tyre-roller setting until you get the same 'roll-down' time. For the test,

ABOVE: *The main advantage of a 'turbo' trainer is that it lets you train when it is dark, wet or cold outside, but using it does require self-discipline.*
RIGHT: *A computer and heart-rate monitor are invaluable for keeping a careful record of your progress.*

ride for three minutes at a series of predetermined intensities, ideally from 60 to 80 per cent of your maximum. Then note your heart rate at the end of the three minute workload: these are your performance scores. In time, you should see a reduction in the heart rate required to produce the same speed or power. It is worth doing the test every week to monitor your progress.

To aid motivation, you can organise group trainer sessions, where you have the opportunity to interact with your fellow cyclists while riding at your own preferred intensity – something not always possible on outdoor group rides.

Heart-rate monitors

As we have already seen, the intensity

at which you are training is an important component of overload. However, it can be difficult to assess exactly how 'hard' a ride is.

Over the years, physiologists who work with athletes have discovered that certain levels of oxygen consumption will bring about improvements in performance. Whilst you cannot train with a machine that

tells you your oxygen consumption, you can use a HRM, and the rate at which your heart beats is a good indicator of the amount of oxygen your body is processing. Although heart rate is not always important, by and large it is a superb means of monitoring and controlling your training.

Your body has no concept of miles per hour: it knows intensity and duration. Say you decide to train at 20 miles per hour on your favourite route. There is a headwind, so you are working extra hard to maintain that speed. The next time, there is a tailwind, so 20 miles per hour is easy. Your heart rate for the first ride could be 170 and for the second 145. In other words, your speed is irrelevant as an indicator of intensity, because speed depends on many variables

apart from how hard your body is working. If, on the other hand, you decide to train at 140-150 beats per minute for an hour, the wind direction makes no difference. Whatever your speed, your body will be working at the right level, and that is what matters.

Some riders and coaches believe that it is possible to go by 'feel' in terms of riding intensity. However, there are flaws in this approach. You know that to improve your endurance you need to do a two-hour 'hard' ride. So off you go, and you ride 'hard'. However, if you had a heart-rate monitor you would see that on the hill where a 'hard' effort usually means 165 beats per minute, you are going 'hard' and yet your heart rate is only 145. Strangely, your body does not seem to be able to work any harder. Now swap sports: you are a racing driver on a practice lap, and you notice that the car's rev counter will not go over 4,000, when normally it is at 9,000, even though you are driving hard. What do you do? You realise that something is wrong with the engine, and you fix it. To translate back into cycling terms, your

body is saying that something is wrong, but without the heart-rate monitor you may not know.

A HRM can also be used to assess the intensity at which you ride when racing, so that you can tailor your training to meet the demands of the event. This is becoming increasingly feasible with the new breed of heart-rate monitors, which record speed, distance, average speed and time in addition to heart rates. Rear wheels (Power-Tap) and cranks (SRM) which measure power can also be used to asses race day effort and help tweak training intensities.

What your monitor will not do is let you compare yourself to your training companions: if your heart rate is ten beats higher than theirs, it means absolutely nothing. Heart rate is an individual thing, and you should compare your rate only with your heart rate on previous comparable rides.

If you do not have a heart-rate monitor, you can still use heart rates in your training. You will need a watch with a second hand or a stopwatch. Find the carotid pulse (under the jaw, a couple of inches from your chin in the direction of your ear) with two fingers. Count the number of times it throbs in fifteen seconds, and multiply that by four. This gives you the number of beats per minute, which tells you how hard you were working immediately before you stopped. With practice, you can do this as you ride, but stopping to take your heart rate is better, as long as you do not pause for more than ten seconds before taking it.

Planning a training programme

Now that you have looked at the theory behind training, training aids and alternatives to on-the-bike training, it is time to start putting together your own personalised training plan.

By working through the four stages outlined below, you should end up with a plan that allows you to make the most effective use of your training time, helps you eliminate weaknesses and sets you on the road to developing the specific fitness you need for success in your chosen cycling events. It may seem obvious, but there is little point in doing just the type of training you are good at: that is simply lazy. Learn to identify what aspects of your fitness and racing need improving and spend time working on them.

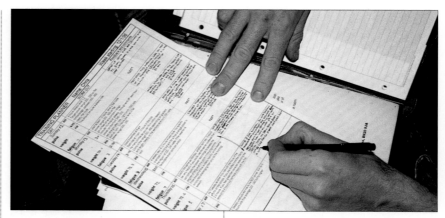

The demands of your goals

As you saw in Chapter 4, certain types of fitness are required for success in the different branches of cycle sport. Take your chosen event and consider the following questions:

• How long do your goal races last?
• Is the intensity consistent or variable?
• What is the lowest intensity with which I will be faced?
• What is the highest intensity with which I will be faced?
• What are all the possible scenarios that can decide the result?

Compare your observations on the event with the descriptions of the six elements of fitness on pages 56–7. Are any of the elements important for race situations that you are likely to come across? If so, the corresponding training session (see pages 78–81) should form a central part of your training plan. For example, if you are a time triallist, you are likely to have to work particularly hard on your intensity threshold; a road racer might need to cover all the elements, while a cyclo-cross rider might concentrate on aerobic power, pain tolerance and muscle power.

Your weaknesses and strengths

Analyse your race performance: when do you lose out to other riders in competition, when do you struggle, what types of courses do you dislike? List everything that you feel prevents you from winning.

Now, using a scale of 1–10 (1 = very poor; 10 = excellent), evaluate yourself objectively on the six aspects of cycle fitness listed below. (These are described in more detail on pages 56–7.) It is even worth getting some input from other riders – maybe you

Component ranking	1	2	3	4	5	6	7	8	9	10
Aerobic capacity (endurance)										
Explosive power (sprinting)										
Muscle power (climbing)										
Intensity threshold (time trialling)										
Aerobic power (short-term endurance)										
Pain tolerance										

ABOVE: *A pro team training together early season.*
FAR LEFT: *A training plan should include areas which you wish to improve, plus your overall objectives for the racing season.*

are not as great a sprinter as you think you are! The main thing is to be honest. Generally, if you enjoy something you are good at it, so if you hate going uphill the chances are that you could usefully spend time improving your climbing skills.

Next, add the elements of fitness in which you rate yourself poorly (scored less than 4) to your list of the competitive situations where you feel that you lose out; make a second list including the elements of fitness you feel that you are good at (scored 8+) and all the race situations where you succeed. These two lists should give you a clear picture of the type of training you need to do.

Your training opportunities

The next stage is to consider how much time you have to train. Calculate how many minutes you can devote to training on each individual day of the week. You will need to take into account your family and work commitments, the climate and daylight hours. Be honest, remembering to deduct the time that it takes to get ready for a ride and to change and shower afterwards, and also any time you need to spend riding clear of traffic and narrow streets before you can commence proper training. Two hours of free time can shrink substantially when you consider all the restrictions that may apply. Often, however, you can liberate more time for training by using a stationary trainer (see page 74).

If you work a shift pattern, you may have plenty of free time on certain days, but lack of sleep would make training dangerous. Your training plan should be arranged to allow for recovery.

Planning your programme

Using all the information you have gathered in the previous three stages, you will need to plan your training programme so that you spend 20 per cent of your time on your strengths, 50 per cent of your time on your weaknesses and 30 per cent on areas in which you are adequate. So if you have ten hours per week to train, spend five hours on weaknesses, two hours on strengths and three hours on everything else. This programme will result in improvements in all aspects of your riding, but will specifically concentrate on eliminating the weaknesses you have identified.

Pages 78–81 show you how you can work on the specific areas of fitness you have targeted, and pages 82–3 include a sample training programme showing how you might put all this information into practice.

The training sessions 1

Once you have worked out your strengths and weaknesses, and the areas on which you need to concentrate, it is time to start work. There are seven types of training session, designed to develop different elements of fitness, which you can incorporate into your training plan.

The various types of session are listed in the box below in increasing order of intensity, with a brief description of their purpose and how they relate to specific cycling situations; on the remainder of pages 78–81, you can see how to undertake them in practice.

How to do the sessions

In order to put into practice some of the seven types of session outlined below, you will need to work out percentages of your maximum heart-rate range (see page 81). Others go on 'feel'. All but two of the session types utilise what is known as 'interval training' – periods of effort separated by recovery intervals when you stay active but at lower intensities.

The important components of an interval-training session are the intensity of each work period, the duration of the work period, the number of work periods (repetitions, or 'reps'), the duration of the rest period between repetitions, the number of times that you do a set of repetitions (sets), and finally the length of the recovery period between sets. Each of the sample sessions outlined on pages 79–80 gives two potential combinations of these variables: this allows you to design a personal training programme to cover all the areas of race fitness you may need to improve, and should also help to keep you motivated.

Many riders think that interval

1 Recovery (REC): this is designed to facilitate recovery by increasing the blood flow through the muscles. This session should feel very easy. Heart rates should be below 60 per cent of your maximum heart-rate range (see page 81).

2 Aerobic capacity (AC): this type of session will help you to build a foundation of endurance and will improve your muscles' ability to use oxygen and fuel efficiently. As fat contributes a greater proportion of your energy needs at this intensity than at higher intensities, these sessions will help you to improve your fat-burning efficiency and to reduce body fat.

3 Explosive power (EP): this is intended to develop the system which supplies energy to the muscles for very short, high-intensity efforts, such as the initial few seconds of an attack in a road race or a track sprint.

4 Muscle power (MP): this is a session aimed at developing strength in the muscles, by stressing them with relatively high pedal resistance. The muscles may become larger, and the nervous system will become capable of sending stronger impulses to the muscles, resulting in an ability to generate greater forces.

5 Intensity threshold (IT): this session will improve your ability to sustain high-intensity exercise for prolonged periods, such as in a time-trial effort. You will be trying to deal with the accumulation of lactic acid, a by-product of high-intensity exercise, which must be recycled or removed from the muscle.

6 Aerobic power (AP): this is a session to stimulate your heart's ability to deliver oxygen to active muscle. The session can help develop speed when done on the flat or climbing power when the efforts are made uphill.

7 Pain tolerance (PT): a painful session with the purpose of developing tolerance to the discomfort that comes from the accumulation of high levels of lactic acid. There is both a physical and a mental adaptation after doing these sessions: when the pain builds up in your legs in the heat of competition, you will be able to keep riding hard.

training just means riding flat out, then resting, then doing it again. This is almost right, but not quite. Never just ride as fast as you can, or you will be able to manage only a couple of attempts before you are too tired to continue. It is better to keep the intensity at a level which allows you to do all the repetitions you had planned. Nine repetitions close to maximum intensity are generally more beneficial than three at maximum. When resting, you should ride around in a low gear to promote recovery. This is much better than just stopping dead, although that is what you may want to do.

You should finish the session if and when you 'lose your form': when your head starts to droop, your shoulders go wobbly and you have to keep getting out of the saddle to keep the gears turning. If you carry on when you are spent, you will just be training yourself to be slow: try to ride in training as you would like to be able to ride in races. Likewise, if you reach the end of your planned session still feeling fresh and with good form, you can do additional intervals, provided you are able to complete them properly.

Components of session	RECOVERY	
	Sample 1	Sample 2
Intensity	< 60% max heart-rate range (MHRR)	
Duration	Between 30 and 60 minutes	
Repetitions	N/A	
Recovery		
Sets	N/A	
Recovery between sets	N/A	

Comments
The intensity should feel light, with no discomfort. It should almost feel too easy to be of benefit.

Components of session	AEROBIC CAPACITY	
	Sample 1	Sample 2
Intensity	65% MHRR	75% MHRR
Duration	3 hours	1–2 hours
Repetitions	N/A	N/A
Recovery	N/A	N/A
Sets	N/A	N/A
Recovery between sets	N/A	N/A

Comments
The main endurance session: you should aim to balance the intensity to enable you to complete the ride. Try not to start off too hard – as a rough guide, the first third of the ride should be comfortable, the middle third uncomfortable and the final third hard.

Components of session	EXPLOSIVE POWER	
	Sample 1	Sample 2
Intensity	Maximal sprint	Maximal, uphill sprint
Duration	10 seconds	6 seconds
Repetitions	12	7
Recovery	3 minutes	2 minutes
Sets	1	2
Recovery between sets	N/A	5 minutes of easy riding (REC) intensity

Comments
The efforts should be maximal, whilst seated, in a high gear. Aim to attack each repetition aggressively, as if sprinting for the finishing line. For the 6-second hill effort, you can get out of the saddle for the initial 2–3 seconds, or the entire repetition. An ideal stationary trainer workout.

The training sessions 2

Components of session	MUSCLE POWER Sample 1	Sample 2
Intensity	Maximal: high gear, low pedal speed	Maximal: high gear, low pedal speed
Duration	20 seconds on steep hill	50 seconds on long gradual hill
Repetitions	6	8
Recovery	1 minute	2 minutes
Sets	2	1
Recovery between sets	3 minutes	N/A

Comments

The effort should feel 'hard', with high resistance from the gearing and incline. As this session is more muscle than cardiovascular related you will find that your heart rate does not go as high as in many of the other sessions. An ideal stationary-trainer workout.

Components of session	INTENSITY THRESHOLD Sample 1	Sample 2
Intensity	85% MHRR	85–90% MHRR
Duration	20 minutes	8 minutes
Repetitions	1	3
Recovery	N/A	4 minutes
Sets	N/A	1
Recovery between sets	N/A	N/A

Comments

The 'time-trial' session: the intensity should feel on the edge – any harder and you will be unable to sustain the effort, any slower and it will be bearable. An ideal stationary-trainer workout.

Components of session	AEROBIC POWER Sample 1	Sample 2
Intensity	Sub-maximal: 90% MHRR +	Maximal
Duration	3 minutes	30 seconds
Repetitions	3	5
Recovery	3 minutes	30 seconds
Sets	2	3
Recovery between sets	5 minutes	5 minutes

Comments

Neither of these sessions is easy, or pain free. You should be riding at an intensity above normal 'race pace'. The sessions can be done on hills, or on the flat. An ideal stationary-trainer workout.

Components of session	PAIN TOLERANCE Sample 1	Sample 2
Intensity	Maximal	Maximal, paced effort
Duration	45 seconds	90 seconds
Repetitions	10	3
Recovery	1 minute	3 minutes
Sets	1	3
Recovery between sets	N/A	6 minutes

Comments

A very painful pair of training sessions, which should by definition be harder than any other. The biggest mistake with these sessions is starting off too hard and being unable to maintain your 'style' or 'form'. An ideal stationary-trainer workout.

HOW IT WORKS

Muscle power sample session 1 consists of two sets of six repetitions, each of 20 seconds followed by one minute of recovery, with three minutes between sets. What you do is this:

20 seconds at maximum, 1 minute recovery
20 seconds at maximum, 1 minute recovery
20 seconds at maximum, 1 minute recovery
20 seconds at maximum, 1 minute recovery
20 seconds at maximum, 1 minute recovery
20 seconds at maximum, 3 minutes recovery

Working out training heart rates

Some of the sample training sessions above and later in this chapter describe intensity in terms of percentages of what is known as your maximum heart-rate range. You can work this out as follows.

First, find your resting heart rate, in beats per minute: this is best done when you wake up in the morning and are still lying down. Next, find your maximum heart rate. One way of doing this is to get a 'guesstimate' by subtracting your age from 220. Alternatively, find your actual maximum: ride gently for ten minutes, start to ride harder for five minutes, then sprint as hard as you can for fifteen seconds uphill. The heart rate you get should be your maximum. (It is important that you do not do this if you suffer from any type of heart problems, or if you have been inactive for a year, or if you are over 35, or if you know of any reason why maximal exercise could be damaging to your health, or if your doctor has ever told you

that you should not exercise maximally. If any of these conditions applies to you, you must get clearance from your doctor before you start to exercise at these intensities.)

Subtract your resting heart rate from your maximum: this gives the heart-rate range, in other words how many beats per minute difference there is between your minimum and maximum. Percentages are calculated in relation to this range: for 60 per cent, you would multiply the range by 0.6, for 80 per cent by

0.8. Finally, add the resting heart rate to the number you end up with. This is your target heart rate.

Although it seems complicated initially, after a couple of attempts you should be able to work it out easily. In fact, you will find you do not need to work out percentages very often.

The graph below shows the heart rates recorded for an aerobic power training session – in this case, three sets of three repetitions.

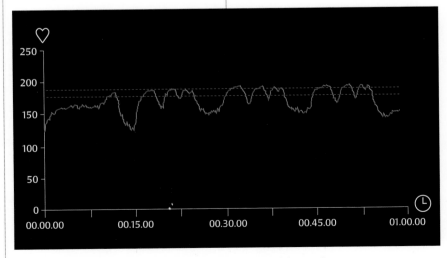

A rider's heart rate as recorded during an aerobic power training session.

A sample training programme

Once you have undertaken the planning processes described on pages 76–7, you will be ready to put together your own tailor-made three-month training plan to take you to the start of the racing season.

To assist you in forming your own plan, below is a sample programme using a total of six hours per week over twelve weeks to accomplish all the training. You need not follow this precise format: it is intended as an example of the way in which you can translate the planning processes and the sample sessions on pages 78–81 into a concrete programme. Any rider who works at the appropriate intensities should gain some fitness through following this programme, but you will see more benefit from a plan designed specifically for your own needs.

The first aim of this three-month training plan is to help you to develop a base of endurance or aerobic fitness that will enable you to last the course. The next phase is designed to build some leg power, increasing the force which the muscles can generate and their ability to keep producing it when they are feeling tired, so that you can go up the hills quickly. This also provides a strength foundation

for the final four-week phase, which concentrates on developing speed to help you get away from your rivals.

You should bear in mind that this is a very generalised plan, aimed at helping everyone

	MON	TUE	WED	THR	FRI	SAT	SUN
1		AC/2		AC/2			AC/2
2		AC/2		IT			AC/2
3		IT		AC/2			IT
4		AC/1		REC/1			AC/1.5
5	REC/1	IT		AP		AC/1	IT
6	REC/1	IT		MP		AC/1.5	AP
7	REC/1	MP		AP		AC/2	MP
8	REC/1	AC/1		IT		REC/1	AC/1.5
9	REC/1	AP		EP		AC/1	PT
10	REC/1	PT		EP		AC/1.5	PT
11	REC/1	EP + PT		AP		AC/2	EP + PT
12		REC/1		EP			AC/1.5

Key: REC/1 = 1-hour recovery ride
AC/2 = 2-hour aerobic capacity ride
EP + AP = an explosive power session followed immediately by an aerobic power session

improve a little. It is perhaps best suited to the rider who currently does a few rides each week as hard as he or she can.

What the plan means

In the first four weeks of the programme, three types of training session are used: aerobic capacity, intensity threshold and recovery. Initially, the training leans towards the aerobic capacity sessions, aiming to develop a base of aerobic fitness on which power and speed can be built as the racing season approaches. You can use hilly terrain for the intensity threshold rides: if you can find big enough hills, the whole work period could take place on a single climb. But avoid anything too steep, as it is important that you pedal fairly quickly, at around 80 revs per minute. On a steep hill you will pedal too slowly, thus training a different physiological system from the one you want to target with this session and making it difficult to reach your target heart rates.

If you have never trained seriously before, you should aim to arrange the sessions so that they never run back to back: try to leave a day between them, especially in the first three weeks. If you have been training pretty regularly and are accustomed to hard riding, you can fit the sessions in around your normal routine, perhaps including the intervals within your usual weekend rides. However, be sure to allow time for rest and recovery. After each session, you should be tired but not worn out. Given time, your body will adapt to the stresses you are placing on it, and you will find the plan easier in the third week than the first. Every fourth week is aimed at allowing your body a period of reduced training to enable it to adapt to the previous three weeks' hard work.

After the first month, your body will have become a little more efficient in its use of oxygen, delivering more to active muscle and using it more effectively in the muscle. In addition, you will be more efficient in your use of fuels, and some structures will be in place to help you to deal with the removal of the waste products which accumulate during hard exercise.

In the second month, you will start to add to this base, developing power as well as maintaining your endurance. This is the time for you to start to prepare more specifically for some of the challenges which the race and your competitors will throw at you. For this month, four different training sessions are used: aerobic capacity, intensity threshold, muscle power and aerobic power.

The final month is concerned with adding speed and power to your armoury, using explosive power, aerobic power and pain tolerance sessions. You will find it a hard month, when recovery is of paramount importance.

Keeping a training diary

It is worth trying to keep a daily training log, including anything that is likely to affect your performance: diet, your previous night's sleep, the weather conditions, resting and

DATE			
RESTING HEART RATE			
LAST NIGHT'S SLEEP	GOOD	FAIR	POOR
DIET	GOOD	FAIR	POOR
TRAINING:			
TIME			
ROUTE			
HEART RATES			
DISTANCE			
CONDITIONS			
OTHER DETAILS			
TRAINING WENT	WELL	OK	BADLY

training heart rates and so on. Exceptionally bad or good rides in future can be better explained if you keep a record of these various factors in your diary. The example above is merely a suggestion.

Race preparation

It is an unfortunate fact that many riders, having devoted a great deal of time and energy to their training, approach competition with no clear plan, overtired and lacking the competitive edge required for success. If you follow these guidelines, you will be able to approach your target events with confidence.

How should you train as a race approaches? First of all, do not make the mistake of trying to train for an event the week before it occurs: race fitness is developed over a month or more. If you know specific details about your rivals or the course, you can design your training around what you know the demands of the race will be.

If it is a very important event, you will want to go to it in peak condition, which involves a process known as 'tapering'. This is a term used to describe a period before a major competition when a rider cuts down his or her training from preparation levels. This phase, which usually follows a long period of hard training and racing, is intended to produce a 'super-adaptation' of the body's systems (see also pages 70–1). In particular, it will help to regenerate the central nervous system and will improve your mental readiness.

A successful taper should therefore involve a gradual reduction of the amount of stress to which you are exposed in training. For many riders, the idea of reducing the time they spend training before a big event is frightening, as they expect to lose much of their fitness. However, as you saw on pages 72–3, overtraining

and a failure to allow the body to adapt prevent many riders from achieving the results in races which their ability and fitness would otherwise suggest are possible.

Prior to tapering, you should have been able to put in at least three and preferably four to five weeks of appropriate intensive training, without interruption. Then comes the period where art meets science, as

you try to maintain your fitness levels while allowing super-adaptation to occur. For well-trained endurance cyclists, the length of the 'unloading' phase should not be more than two weeks (to prevent de-training), with ten days being the best bet for a one-off peak. A four-day taper will allow you to be fresh and sharp for an event without a true peaking of condition.

Riders who are aware of tapering

ABOVE: *Team talk before a race start.*
LEFT: *A rider on a race start line taking the last vital sips of an energy drink as he focuses on the race ahead.*
RIGHT: *A soigneur handing out race food to his team riders before the start of a road race.*

in a car. Note hills, difficult descents and corners, and any potholes and manhole covers which may cause problems such as punctures.

For road races, look for the best places to attack or to recover after an attack, and make sure you know where the wind is likely to be strongest and on what parts of the course you can get shelter from it.

Post-race analysis

Once the race is over, analyse what went right or wrong, and why. Where did you lose out, what would you do

as a principle often make a simple mistake when trying to apply it: they eliminate all the intensity from their training before the race. A taper must involve the same intensities as your normal training, but a reduction in the duration of the efforts. Taper periods are not the same as rest periods.

For less important events, you simply need to ensure that you are fresh and well rested. The week immediately preceding any race should be spent refining your riding skills, allowing your body to recover and eating well. Again, you should aim to reduce the total time spent training, but to keep the intensity as high as normal until a couple of days before the event. You should then have a rest day two days before the race, and a short, easy

endurance workout the preceding day. Too many riders train too hard during the week between races and are left feeling tired and unable to perform as well as they expected.

Race reconnaissance

When you arrive at the event, you should allow yourself time to look over the course, either on the bike, perhaps as part of your warm-up, or

differently next time, and can you improve on anything? Be fair, and try to stay clear of bringing other people into the evaluation. 'They', 'he', 'she' and 'it' seldom really keep you from a higher placing. Do not forget to look back at your diet and the amount of sleep you had in the days leading up to the race: these are two factors which are often at the root of seemingly inexplicable poor performances.

Easy improvements

Having seen the process behind planning a training programme, it may help you to know that there are also some 'quick fixes' for achieving a little more speed. Here are seven simple tips to work on next time you are searching for extra performance.

Whilst most riders are aware of the importance of diet in performance, few realise the need for extra water intake during the day.

We lose water through sweating, and also through expired air, especially in the cold, so if you are active you can be sure that you need to increase your fluid intake – off the

bike as well as when riding. You should aim to drink five or six glasses of water per day, apart from other drinks. Whilst your body is able to extract water from various other drinks and foods, it absorbs pure water more easily. You will be surprised what difference an increase in water intake can make to the way you perform.

Testing your fitness

If you train with a heart-rate monitor, this is an easy way of testing your fitness as it progresses (or declines). As well as the monitor, you will need a cycle computer and a long hill. Ride between two points on the hill, such as lamp posts or gates, at a set speed, for instance twelve miles per hour, and note your heart rate as you pass the second point. On the same hill, at the same speed, and between the same two points, you should see a fall in heart rate as your fitness improves – provided, of course, a strong headwind is not blowing you down the hill! As the heart and muscles become more efficient with training, you need fewer heart beats to deliver the necessary amount of oxygen and fuel for the same effort.

A 'quickie' training ride

If work or other commitments leave you with limited training time, you may wonder what to do with occasional brief sessions. An 'out-and-back' ride could be the answer. If, for example, you have 50 minutes of on-the-bike time, ride away from home for 25 minutes, including ten minutes at a moderate pace for a warm-up. Then turn round and try to get home in less than 25 minutes. You will have to ride quite hard to overhaul your

slower ten-minute warm-up speed, ride up any hills you rode down, and so on. This is a good, hard ride, making use of limited time.

Increasing pedalling speed

Stay off the big chainring in winter. Try to develop pedalling speed rather than plodding strength. Because it is difficult for 'plodders' to increase their pedalling speed in the same big gear, they rarely improve. By using lower gears at higher revs, you make more use of aerobic muscle fibres, which are more efficient over long periods and do not tire easily. They can, with training, turn bigger gears at high revs: as your fitness improves, you can increase the gears being used. However, the muscle fibres which

TYRE PRESSURES

Whilst this is not quite a fitness tip, it is a 'faster' tip. Check your tyre pressure: if it is too low, pumping it up to the correct pressure will do wonders for your speed. You will be surprised how much faster road tyres are at eight bar (115psi), as opposed to the five bar (75psi) for which many riders settle.

churn big gears tire easily and cannot adapt well to faster pedal speeds.

Change of routine

If you have reached a plateau in your fitness and have started to wallow around at one level of ability, try riding your normal training routes in

reverse. Those hills you love to zoom down will stretch your climbing ability, and viewing the scenery from the opposite angle will undoubtedly refresh your mind.

Identifying your aims

Before a training ride, stop and ask yourself what you hope to achieve from it. Too many riders simply go out on their bikes, with little purpose. Set an aim for the session and go for it. For example, if you want to improve your sprinting ability, include ten or fifteen ten-second sprints in your ride. Use slight inclines for sprinting strength and power, and slight descents for sprinting speed.

Beating boredom

If you find you become bored when you ride on the 'turbo', dig out old videos of the Tour de France or other races, and watch while you train. Try to copy the action of the riders on the screen. For example, when you watch a sprint finish, sprint on the turbo; while watching a bunch roll along, take it easy; and when watching a climb use top gear and get out of the saddle to keep it turning.

CHAPTER 6

Buying a bike – the frame and fit

Racing bikes are specifically designed for efficiency, both in their mechanical structure and as a means for your body to achieve its maximum power output. But even the most expensive bike will not be

efficient if its frame or components are the wrong size for the rider: in fact, it could be a liability. A relatively inexpensive bike, chosen with care, and perhaps with a little fine tuning to perfect the fit, can take the beginner a very long way; it is often

difficult to see tangible benefits from the exotic end of the market. If you read the whole of this chapter, and Chapter 7, before buying, you should avoid expensive mistakes.

Introducing the racing bike

Before you can make any choices about your frame and fit, you must first consider the purpose of the bike as a whole. Racing bikes vary greatly according to the type of event, and the more you specialise the more you are likely to spend.

A training bike takes the wear and tear of daily use. Mudguards may be a good idea, as road spray is no fun even for the most hardened cyclist.

As with many other items, the hard-earned cash you spend on a bike brings great dividends up to a point, but then the rule of diminishing returns applies the more you spend. Expensive fine tuning is really of benefit only to the experienced cyclist. So what bike should you settle for?

The basic racing bike

Most major manufacturers offer a full range of road bikes, and it's always a good idea to invest as much as you can from the outset, as upgrading from the entry level is sometimes a futile exercise, as the components are often more expensive than the bike itself.

In general it's not a good idea to go for the very low-end models, as these are really not suitable for semi-serious cycling. On a basic budget you will probably find a number of decent aluminium-framed bikes on offer, many even with carbon forks. These are versatile entry-level bikes, which are ideal for starting out in the sport and even for club events.

But as with everything in life, the more serious you become the better your equipment must become, and as you progress you will find your own niche and get to know what suits you. Your original bike is rarely dead money, as a training/winter bike is always a wise investment, and this should fit the bill nicely.

A wise policy is to look for the previous year's models – specifications change rapidly, but don't improve greatly; so in spring and autumn there are always plenty of end-of-line offers available. Second-hand bikes are also often a good bet, but always look for potential frame dents and damage, and telltale creaks and bangs. If you find these walk away.

An entry-level racing bike should provide all you need for your first season's racing: efficiency, a good fit and reliability.

A daunting array of similar-looking road frames: choose one with great care.

As you compare various models of bike, you will find that the specification divides into four main areas: the frame, the wheels, the groupset (the transmission, braking and bearing components) and the finishing kit (the handlebars, saddle and stem). These parts of the bike are generally manufactured by specialist companies; the frame manufacturer or importer simply puts them together and sells the complete bike. Some bike companies use 'own-brand' components with their name or a name exclusive to them, but they never make more than a very few of these themselves.

Do not be too deterred if an off-the-peg bike is not exactly what you want: better bike shops will normally change components such as saddles, stems and pedals for you. Although this will probably add to the cost, it can be cheaper than getting the job

Try and get out on training rides with your local 'chain gang'. Do not worry if you do not have the 'right' bike – it is more important to build up your fitness.

done later, as the shop should reimburse you for the original parts.

Buying a frame

Towards the more expensive end of the market, frames are often bought alone rather than as part of a complete bike. The frame can then be built to your exact size. Acquiring the components separately and building up your own bike is often more expensive than buying a similar complete bike, but it offers you the chance to choose exactly the specification you want. Skill, experience and special tools are needed to assemble a bike properly; having a shop build it up for you is recommended, but adds further to the final cost. Some larger dealers specialise in a 'pick-and-mix' approach, offering various frames with different component packages. These can sometimes offer very good value, as well as more exactly meeting your needs.

Training bikes

You will also need to think about a training bike, on which you may do the bulk of your riding. The ideal is to have a separate bike, or at least a second set of wheels, to avoid damage to your expensive racing equipment. Although you can use any bike to gain fitness, a training bike with an identical fit and similar handling to your racing bike is an advantage, so that the transition between them on race days is not too disorientating.

The racing frame: the heart of the bike

The frame and forks are collectively known as the frameset. The material, design and construction of the frameset determine the efficiency, handling, comfort and general feel of your bike, so choosing a frame is the most important decision you will make.

There is no perfect bike frame, only the best set of compromises for your particular needs, and even these can differ from race to race. When buying, you will need to think in general terms about the issues that are most important for you, and then pay some attention to the fine detail; you may need to balance this against the bike package as a whole.

Frame weight and stiffness

Frame stiffness is a priority for many riders. The main benefit of a stiff frame is to keep the wheels in precise alignment: this aids cornering, so is important for tight criterium racing and descending. A stiffer frame is also often said to be more efficient at transforming energy into forward movement, but this effect is almost

wholly psychological, as the gains are minute. On the other hand, if a stiff frame makes you feel better, so that you ride your best, or if others feel inferior on less stiff machines, then it is a genuine advantage.

Stiffness is dependent on several things, including the frame material and also the diameter, length, gauge (wall thickness) and shape of the

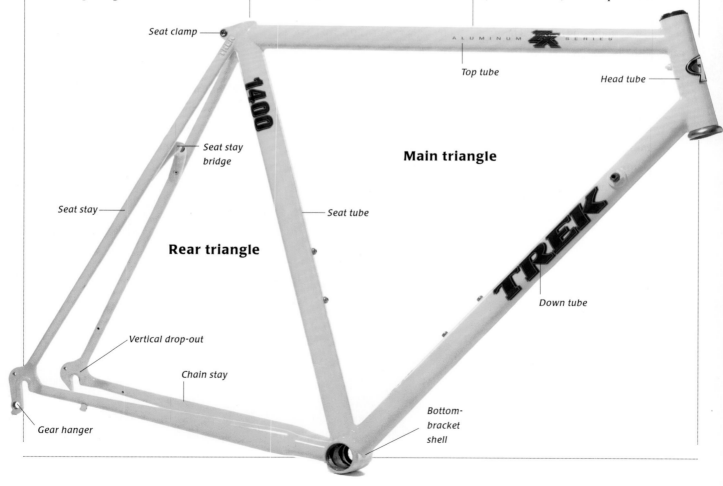

Seat clamp

Top tube

Head tube

1400

Seat stay bridge

Main triangle

Seat stay

Seat tube

Rear triangle

Down tube

Vertical drop-out

Chain stay

Gear hanger

Bottom-bracket shell

tubing used. (Tube shape can increase stiffness in a particular plane, but will not make a frame stiffer overall.) Different frame materials (see pages 94–7) vary in springiness for a given weight, but on the whole greater stiffness is achieved by using either oversize or thicker-gauge tubing, which tends to mean increased weight. Smaller frames are stiffer than large ones, so they can be built more lightly. Whilst weight-saving is helpful for acceleration and hill climbing, this must be balanced against losses due to frame flexing, so a fine compromise is called for.

'Road shock' can be an issue with stiff frames: because more shock is transmitted to the rider, such frames are less comfortable, which is an important consideration if you are intending to ride endurance events.

Frame failure

The force required to pull a material apart is known as its ultimate tensile strength (UTS). This is really important only in a crash, as a frame material with a lower UTS will be more liable to break or bend. However, most materials with a higher UTS are used in thinner sections, this saves weight, but the tubes are less stiff and more liable to denting. Metal fatigue is a separate issue: over time, the repeated stresses of pedalling and the vibration from the road surface bring about millions of flexes on the frame, effectively bending it to and fro and causing it to break. This is not normally an issue with well-built steel

Horizontal drop-outs are still used on some frames. These should have adjustable limiting stops to make wheel alignment easy.

and titanium frames, but it can be with aluminium and carbon fibre. Sudden changes in any material's section or thickness create a focus for stresses known as a 'stress riser'; the fatigue then builds up very much more quickly, leading to cracking and rapid failure. Metal fatigue is also the most common form of component failure for the same reasons.

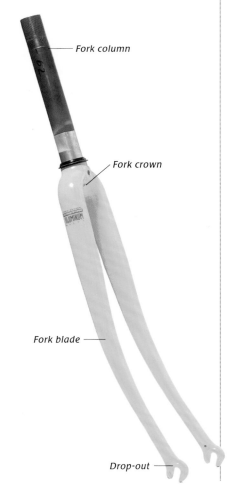

Fork column

Fork crown

Fork blade

Drop-out

FRAME FACTS

FRAMES are built with a 130mm dropout width suitable for eight, nine or ten-speed hubs (see pages 110–11). Most steel frames except those made of Reynolds 753 tubing can be reset to 130mm, but this is a job for a professional.
DROP-OUTS Vertical drop-outs are the most common: they make wheel fitting easier. Horizontal drop-outs allow some adjustment, making it easier to continue if you buckle the wheel. Some front fork drop-outs have 'safety' lips. These make wheel changing tedious (see page 148).
BRAZE-ONS are the small fittings designed for mounting some components. Originally brazed onto frames, they can be soldered, welded or glued. Most frames provide the basics, such as cable guides and stops, but the number of bottle-cage mounts varies. A chain hanger makes maintenance easier.
HEADSETS Two types of headset (steering bearing) arrangement are found on off-the-peg racing bikes. The traditional style uses a different fork steerer to the threadless (Aheadset) style headsets increasingly used on road bikes. Threadless headsets and stems save some weight and bearing adjustment is easier but handlebar height adjustment is trickier. (see p119).

Steel and aluminium frames

Frames may be built from a bewildering array of materials, using a variety of construction methods. An understanding of these will help you to make the best choice.

Ordinary high-tensile steel is commonly used in the cheapest sports bikes for the seat and chain stays and sometimes the forks. Being less strong than alloyed steel, it is used in thicker gauges, which adds weight. It also gives a ride with a 'dead' feel.

In order to make it stronger, steel can be alloyed with traces of other elements. Most good-quality cycle tubing is made from a chrome–molybdenum alloy usually known as

CrMo; manganese–molybdenum tubes, manufactured only by Reynolds, are very similar. Such alloy tubing can be used in a thinner gauge in order to save weight. Good-quality tubes are 'butted' (made thicker) at their ends to compensate for the loss of strength caused by the stress and heat from welding. As a minimum, you should aim to buy a frame made from butted CrMo or Reynolds 531 throughout, including the forks. The typical weight of a steel frameset is 2.4–3.0kg.

High-tech tubes such as Reynolds 753 and Columbus Nivacrom and Thermacrom are more sophisticated: because they are heat-treated to increase their UTS, they can be made thinner still. These tubes are more prone to denting, however, particularly when oversize. Reynolds tubing, 853, is unique in that its strength increases after brazing or welding, and its hard surface reduces the risk of denting.

Brazing in progress: this is the traditional way of joining steel tubes.

Alloy steel offers a good balance between stiffness, strength, weight, adaptability and cost, and it remains the favourite material of custom builders. It is also the easiest to repair. Many experienced cyclists prefer the 'feel' of the best steel frames over other materials: the bike responds as you pedal hard and feels lively, yet it has the ability to absorb road shocks.

Aluminium

Aluminium is widely used for the construction of road bike frames at all prices. The more expensive ones are significantly lighter than even the best steel frames yet will still offer reliable service. The cheaper ones offer no

Versatile steel: aerodynamic and 'star' section down tubes from Columbus and a curved seat tube from Reynolds, used for a shorter rear triangle.

advantages to riders over their steel equivalents. The UTS of pure aluminium is low, so it is mixed with other elements to produce a range of alloys. The alloys known as 5,000, 6,000 and 7,000 series are commonly used for bike frames. Some alloys need to be heat-treated to realise

The gear hanger of some aluminium and carbon-fibre frames bolts on, making this vulnerable part of the frame replaceable.

....

their full strength, a process available only to mass-producers. A drawback is that frames made from these alloys cannot be repaired. The best aluminium tubes, notably those produced by Easton and Cannondale, are butted.

Aluminium alloys have a low fatigue limit and will bend more under load. To counter this, manufacturers use larger-diameter tubes, which reduce frame flex and hence the likelihood of fatigue. This means that, despite aluminium being one third the weight of steel, oversize aluminium frames are only about 300g lighter than the lightest steel frames. They are, however, much stiffer than steel, and in fact often give a rather unforgiving ride, which some riders

find too harsh on poorer road surfaces. The typical weight of an aluminium frameset is 1.9–2.5kg.

Frame construction methods

Brazing is the traditional way of joining steel tubes. Mitred tubes are usually held together by 'lugs', which are heated to about 900°C before melted bronze is fed into the join. The lugs should have a tapered, stress-dispersing profile, rather than resembling plumbing joints. For high-quality steel alloys, silver solder is usually used, at lower temperatures, reducing the loss of strength. It takes great skill to make a good lugged frame but it makes for an extremely reliable result.

Fillet brazing with melted bronze joins the tubes without lugs, allowing for a wider range of frame geometries.

TIG welding is a high-tech method used by many frame builders, especially for mass-produced steel frames and for most aluminium and titanium frames. Some tubing is specially designed for TIG welding, with shorter butts to save weight.

TOP: *A lugged joint: these are now used less for production frames, but are still common on hand-built frames;*
ABOVE: *A cutaway section of a perfectly lugged and brazed joint. The tubes must be mitred together with no gaps, and the bronze must penetrate the joint fully.*

....

Poor TIG welding looks uneven: individual blobs of weld may melt into the parent material, thinning and weakening it. This results in an increased risk of frame failure.

LEFT: *TIG welding in progress. The mitred tubes are joined together by a filler rod (electrode) which melts when it comes into contact with the frame. An inert gas shield repels impurities.*
RIGHT: *TIG welding is distinguished by small blobs of weld, which should join neatly together.*

Exotic materials

Aerospace materials are increasingly being used for bike frames. If the price does not deter you, the need to live up to the bike's image may – or alternatively it may spur you on to greater things!

Merlin's titanium frames being welded. This must be done in scrupulously clean conditions, as contamination will seriously flaw the weld quality.

The best titanium alloys are almost as strong as steel yet only half the weight. Fatigue strength is also excellent. Taking only strength into account then, a frame built from titanium can be much lighter than one built from steel. A typical titanium frameset weight (with forks of an alternative material) is 1.7–2.3kg. However strength is not the only property which needs to be taken into account. A frame that rides well also has to be stiff enough to ensure that the front wheel goes exactly where you lean it and is not deflected by bumps in the road

or by the rider sprinting. Titanium bends more for a given load than steel if a tube of the same diameter, wall thickness, shape and length is used. In order to create a frame that is similarly stiff to a good steel frame, slightly larger diameter tubes are used to restore some of the stiffness lost by the more flexible titanium. In some cases ovalising is also used – the benefits of this are rather doubtful.

As a result of the properties of titanium and the manner in which they are used titanium frames generally

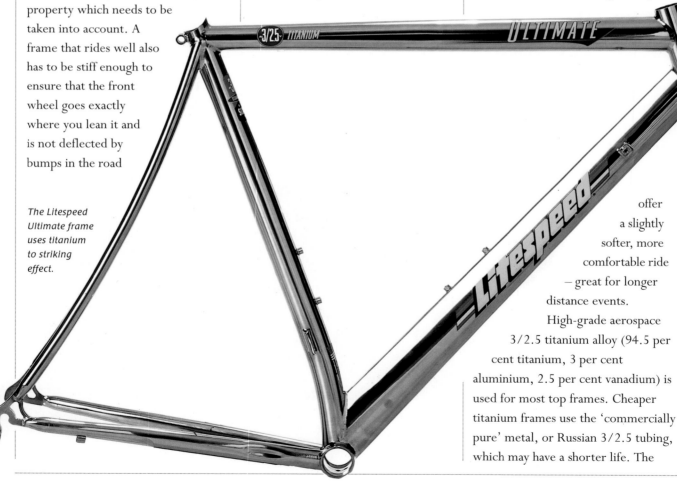

The Litespeed Ultimate frame uses titanium to striking effect.

offer a slightly softer, more comfortable ride – great for longer distance events.

High-grade aerospace 3/2.5 titanium alloy (94.5 per cent titanium, 3 per cent aluminium, 2.5 per cent vanadium) is used for most top frames. Cheaper titanium frames use the 'commercially pure' metal, or Russian 3/2.5 tubing, which may have a shorter life. The

6/4 titanium alloy (90 per cent titanium, 6 per cent aluminium, 4 per cent vanadium) is harder and stronger than 3/2.5I.

Carbon fibre

Weight for weight, carbon fibres on their own are much stronger and more rigid than steel, but only in one plane. The fibres are layered in epoxy resin to make a composite material, in such a way as to give strength and rigidity where needed. This makes for highly versatile, strong, light and stiff frames,

A specialist operation: a vacuum oven is used by Fibre Lyte in order to set a carbon-fibre frame.

which are usually designed to give an absorbent ride. Kevlar fibres are added to make the material less brittle: if it breaks, it will do so less suddenly.

However, the surface is relatively soft, and may become pitted or gouged; bare cables, for instance, should be routed carefully to avoid them wearing into the frame. Frames involved in an accident should be checked very carefully. The layers of carbon fibre may become delaminated which would not be apparent on a cursory inspection. Damaged frames can be repaired, but this must be done by an expert.

Carbon-fibre frames may be constructed by using epoxy glues to join close-fitting frame tubes or frame elements, inside 'lugs' usually made of aluminium alloy or carbon fibre.

However, carbon fibre comes into its own in monocoque (one-piece) forms, as extra fibres can easily be laid to increase stiffness and improve aerodynamics at any point throughout the structure. Not all 'monocoques' are really made in one piece: they often consist of several elements bonded together.

Frames using carbon-fibre composite tubes are usually the least expensive. The Trek OCLV is one of the more advanced of these. The typical carbon-fibre frameset weight is 1.9–2.4kg.

Carbon-fibre forks are usually fitted to titanium and aluminium bikes, as they have great advantages in terms of strength, weight, stiffness and shock-absorbency.

Some manufactures now use a mix of materials on their high-end frames, partly for style, but it can have its benefits. Titanium and aluminium main frames with carbon rear seat stays is the most common mix; this lightens and stiffens the frame a little. Other manufacturers also strategically position small elastomer and Kevlar inserts into their frames, which takes out a small amount of the road shock.

Frame design and purpose

The overall design of a bike frame varies according to the type of cycling for which it is intended and the size and strength of the rider. The handling of a well-maintained bike is determined largely by its frame geometry. Cyclists' preferences vary, so you should choose what suits you.

All road-racing bikes should have similar steering characteristics, so that all riders hold the same line when cornering in a bunch: not doing so can cause crashes. Typical road-racing geometry, with its highly responsive steering, may not be suitable for time trialling, however, especially in long events such as twelve-hour time trials and when using tri-bars, as it can require too much concentration. For such uses, 'slower' steering is preferable.

The main factor affecting the predictability of a bike's steering and its stability is its 'trail', shown in the diagram below left. This varies greatly between different types of bike; even two racing bikes may have significantly different trail figures, depending on the use for which they are intended.

For greatest accuracy, trail is normally calculated by trigonometry from the head-tube angle, fork offset and wheel radius:

$$\frac{\text{wheel radius}}{\text{Tan head angle}} - \frac{\text{fork offset}}{\text{Sin head angle}}$$

A shallow head angle with a large offset can produce the same trail as a steep head angle with a short fork offset. Trail is also reduced when smaller wheels are used. For convenience, trail figures obtained from typical head angles and fork offsets are shown in the diagram below, which should also make the following points clearer and help you to decide what frame geometery you need.

Finding the desired combination of steering and stability can be done by

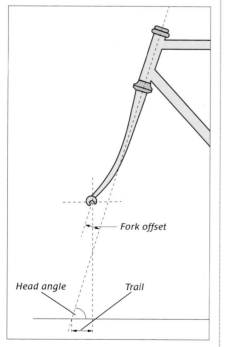

'Trail' is the distance between the point where an imaginary line continued from the steering axis meets the ground, and the point directly under the front hub.

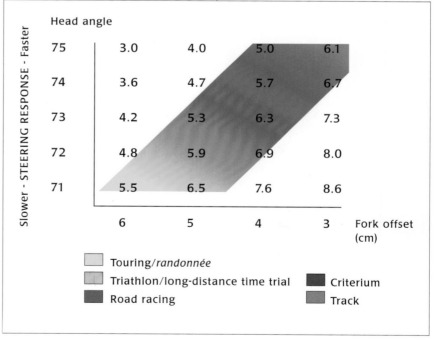

Head angle and fork offset are usually given by the manufacturer, but trail figures less often: this chart is intended to help you to work them out. The coloured zones indicate suitable trail and head-angle figures for bikes intended for different uses. These figures are for 700C wheels: trail figures for 650C wheels are 18 per cent less than quoted.

Straight and raked forks behave in similar ways.

looking carefully at the trail and the head-tube angle. Generally, high-speed stability increases with greater trail, while with a steep head-tube angle the steering is more responsive. Bikes with both characteristics can be steered almost exclusively by feel, and are ideal for sprints or a tight criterium circuit.

A shallower head angle makes the bike less responsive when you turn the bars, which is again advantageous for high-speed stability. A longer fork offset is required to achieve a suitable trail, and this in turn offers greater fork flexibility and thus greater comfort.

Raked (curved) forks and power (straight) forks have very similar handling characteristics, as they produce the same trail figures for a given fork offset. Any minor differences come from the fact that raked forks are better at absorbing shock, while power forks may resist sideways forces better, making cornering more positive. Track fork blades traditionally have a round, rather than oval, cross-section.

Design details

Various criteria, including rider fit and the type of racing for which the bike is intended, may affect elements of the frame design. For example, the bottom-bracket height (measured from the centre of the bottom-bracket axle to the ground) is not always the same. A higher bottom bracket reduces the risk of grounding the pedals whilst cornering but it also raises the centre of gravity. Thus a bike designed for endurance events may have a lower bottom bracket than one for criteriums. Typically, the height is 27cm, but the thickness of the tyres may affect this by up to 7mm. The type of pedals used and the crank length also affect ground clearance.

Mudguards

If you wish to fit mudguards for training, or to ride Audax events, where they are compulsory, you will need a minimum gap of 7mm between the tyre tread and the nearest points of the fork crown, seat tube, seat-stay bridge and chain-stay bridge. As you may want to use tyres with a section of up to 28mm for such purposes, it is a good idea to check the measurements with these tyres fitted. Remember also that the clearance between your feet and the front wheel will be less than normal, causing possible interference. Ideally, for fitting mudguards your frame should have threaded eyes on the drop-outs; however, P-shaped clips can also be used. SKS narrow-section mudguards are a popular choice, as are the special aluminium Salmon guards, which can be fitted to frames with closer clearances.

Tyre clearances

Some racing frames are made with minimal space between the tyre tread and frame, reducing the lengths of tubing required, saving weight and reducing frame flex. However, changing your wheel will be easier if the clearance is not too tight for the tyre you have selected.

Some outright racing bikes have minimal, 'cigarette-paper' clearances between the tyre tread and seat tube. Wheels may need to be fitted with the tyre deflated.

The frame for your body

To obtain a good fit you must have a frame of the right dimensions, even though there is some room for adjustment in the components. Read the following pages before deciding what you need. A knowledgeable dealer who can correctly assess your position is a great help.

To avoid the possibility of injury, there should be at least a 2.5cm gap between the bike's top tube and your crotch as you stand over the middle part of the top tube. The 'stand-over height' given by the manufacturers is measured from the ground to the top of the top tube. Generally, frame size is the distance from the centre of the bottom-bracket axle to the intersection of the seat tube and the top of the top tube, but it can also be measured to the top-tube centre line, or it may be simply the seat-tube length. On standard road frames with a horizontal top tube, the seat tube length should be between 65% and 69% of your inside-leg length.

More important is the length of the top tube, as measured between the centre of its intersections with the seat and head tubes. Many manufacturers use compact frame designs of varying types; these make for lighter weights and stiffer rides, and although they often look small remember that it's the top tube length that's crucial. On compact frames this should be measured from the centre of the top of the head tube – horizontally and parallel to the ground – to the centre of the seat tube (or seat post on sloping top tubes).

Most frames are aimed at 'average-sized' men, but many manufacturers

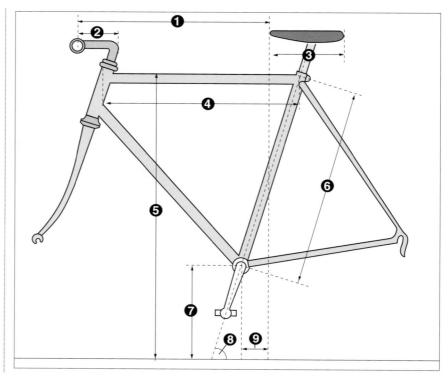

The critical dimensions for frame fit.
1 *Overall reach;* **2** *Handlebar stem length;* **3** *Saddle fore and aft adjustment;* **4** *Top-tube length;* **5** *Stand-over height;* **6** *Seat-tube length;* **7** *Bottom-bracket height;* **8** *Seat-tube angle;* **9** *Saddle setback.*

now also produce woman-specific ranges of bikes. These generally have shorter top tubes and more female-friendly components, such as shallower bars and brake levers, shorter cranks, and comfy saddles.

Almost all racing bikes are designed primarily for the 'average' man. Although some adjustment can be made to saddle position and handlebar stem length to determine the overall reach to

the bars, this might compromise fit and weight distribution in other ways.

The seat-tube angle determines the limits of the saddle's setback, as measured horizontally to the centre of the bottom-bracket axle from a plumbline from the saddle tip. Whatever the seat-tube angle, the same length of top tube and handlebar stem will be required to maintain the reach. If, on the other hand, the saddle is adjusted on the seat post to alter the setback, the handlebar stem length will need to be altered correspondingly. Taken to extremes, this can have an adverse effect on weight distribution and therefore handling. If after experimentation you find that your most comfortable and efficient riding position is with the saddle at its furthest forward or back, you would benefit from a frame with a different seat-tube angle. A steeper seat tube also increases the clearance between the toe and front wheel, as a

Straight-through seat pillars position the saddle cradle directly above the pillar, creating a seat angle two degrees steeper than conventional seat-post designs.

greater proportion of the top tube is in front of the bottom bracket.

A typical seat-tube angle is 72–73 degrees, which suits men of an average build for road racing and hill climbing. Weight distribution, riding style and personal preference are the important considerations. Male riders with lighter shoulders and women, who tend to have heavier hips, normally benefit from steeper seat tubes, as the weight distribution is improved.

A very steep angle of 74–78 degrees is sometimes used by triathletes, as it makes leaning well

forward on tri-bars easier. The angle between the body and the legs is easier to maintain, but beyond a certain point pedalling efficiency may be reduced.

Going custom?

Production bikes do vary in dimensions, and even for those riders who are not 'average' a carefully chosen bike, with a suitable stem length, may be a good, and relatively cheap, bet. On the other hand, a custom frame, built to meet your exact riding and physical needs, can prove really worthwhile. Choose a custom builder with care, checking his

TOP: *A good custom builder can build a correctly proportioned bike for anyone.*
LEFT: *The Cannondale 'Compact' frames have dimensions better suited to most women.*

or her reputation for the type of bike in which you are interested. Give detailed information about your riding style and needs, but be guided by what the builder has to say.

Small frames

Some 'small' bikes are not genuinely so: they simply have a shorter seat tube and a higher bottom bracket! Correct shorter length cranks make the designing of small frames easier. See page 115 for crank length recommendations. Very small frames often have a shallow head angle, with, usually, a correspondingly longer fork offset to avoid the toe getting in the way of the front wheel: this can affect the handling. Smaller 650C wheels enable better geometry to be used, but see the comments on pages 122–3.

The basic racing position

The best racing position is the one that is most physically and aerodynamically efficient, but is also comfortable for the duration of the event. Correct fit is also vital in order to avoid pain, strains and injury.

As we are all different, any theory about position is only a starting point. Experiment, and let experience guide you. A new position may feel strange at first, so give yourself time to become accustomed to it. Remember that one adjustment or component change will affect other elements of the position: for example, a higher saddle increases the bar reach. (See pages 160–1 for how to make the adjustments.)

A correct riding position in which you can relax is essential to riding fast and efficiently.

Saddle height

This is the most critical measurement. As a starting point, adjust the height of the saddle so that with your shoe correctly positioned on the pedal (see pages 116–7), and with the pedal at its lowest position, there is a slight bend in your knee. A saddle that is too high is likely to give the rider pain behind the knee, and he or she may compensate by rolling off the sides of the saddle when pedalling. A too low saddle can cause pain in the front of the knee. Bear in mind that changing shoes and/or pedals can alter the effective saddle height.

Studies have found that a distance of between 105 and 109 per cent of your inside-leg measurement from the centre of the saddle top to the pedal platform is best. To find your inside-leg measurement, wear racing clothing and shoes and stand against a wall, with your feet about 18cm apart. Ask a helper to hold a thin hardback book against your crotch until it is just uncomfortable, then to put a mark on the wall at the bottom corner of the book; you can add the length of the book to the height of the mark above the floor.

If after two weeks of regular riding you are happy with your initial

If you put your heel on the pedal, your leg should be just straight.

· ·

position, try working your saddle up to 109 per cent of your inside-leg measurement, raising it 5mm every two weeks until you have found your most efficient height.

Saddle-clamp adjustment

Saddle setback and angle adjustments are made by moving the saddle frame within the seat post's saddle clamp. The setback will largely be determined by the frame design (see pages 100–1), but the clamp allows some fine adjustment. It is important

to experiment, bearing in mind the effect on the reach. The saddle should be completely flat: if it is tipped down, your arms and back could be strained, although a very slight tip is used by some triathletes and time triallists in a very stretched-out position. Tipped up, the saddle can hurt or cause numbness in the groin. An incorrectly positioned saddle can also lead to saddle sores and general discomfort. (See pages 160–1 for how to adjust the saddle position.)

Handlebar position

Bar reach and height should combine to give the rider a flat back when the 'drop' part of the bars is used (if the rider can manage it – some cannot). The upper arms should be at 90 degrees to the shoulders, and the forearms parallel to the ground. Too short a reach causes the back to arch and can hinder breathing; too long 'locks' the elbows, so that they have no give, and results in back strain. When trying out the reach, take into account the different positions you use for holding the handlebars.

In general, have the bars as low as you find comfortable: start with the tops of the bars a little lower than the top of the saddle, gradually easing yourself further down. If you have long arms, a long torso and/or an aggressive riding stance, you will need lower bars.

If you do need to adjust the reach, you can of course achieve this by altering the saddle setback (bearing in mind the other consequences of doing this). Alternatively, you will need a stem of a different length. A longer

BRAKE-LEVER POSITION: The ideal reach from ❶ the hoods and ❷ the drops. Raising the lever will make it easier to reach from the hoods, while lowering it brings it closer to the drops. A compromise may be needed. Shimano brake levers tend to suit small hands better than Campagnolo ones do.

· ·

stem will put more of your weight over the front wheel and make the steering slower. A shorter stem will do the opposite, and can make the bike feel more skittish.

The lower, flat part of the bars should be between parallel and at an angle of 10 degrees to the ground. The brake-lever position will depend on the bar angle: after setting the bars you may need to reposition the levers so that they can be reached more comfortably. (See pages 158–9 for how to adjust the brake levers.)

Special positions

Tri-bars have become a virtual requirement for time trialling ever since Greg LeMond used them to stunning effect in his 1989 Tour de France victory. If you are upgrading your bike for time trialling or triathlons, these are a top priority, just behind clipless pedals.

The purpose of tri-bars is to achieve the smallest and most aerodynamic profile. The faster you go, the more effective they are. However, they must not reduce your ability to pedal or breathe, and they are not permitted in road racing. They are best fitted to a bike with slower steering and greater trail, so that road irregularities do not throw you.

Tri-bars are normally clamped to your existing drop bars, but sleeker, special stem/tri-bar units are also available from ITM. Smaller frames may require an arm-rest riser kit; models that clamp below the bars are better if the frame is a little large for you. If you have unusually long or short arms, you will require bars with plenty of adjustment. Most models allow you to fit fingertip bar-end gear levers (made by Campagnolo and Shimano) or Gripshifts, often seen on mountain bikes, where the gear-changing mechanism is incorporated into a hand grip. Adaptors are also available to fit down-tube levers. Before buying any handlebar, stem or fitting, check with your dealer that it is compatible with your existing equipment, as clamp sizes vary.

When using tri-bars for the first time, start with your elbows wide apart enough for you to feel confident. Practise on quiet roads before you use tri-bars in competition. A little at a

time, you should bring in the arm rests until your elbows almost touch. Learn to lower the chin to fill the gap between the upper arms, and remember to keep your knees in. Try to develop the suppleness to adopt a flat back: you may need to fit a longer handlebar stem to do this. Avoid slipping towards the point of the saddle: move it forwards if necessary and if there is room for adjustment. Experiment with the angle of the bars, which should be between 15 degrees and 30 degrees to the ground: the lower you get, the faster you will go.

Low-profile bars

These provide a position equivalent to or lower than the drops of conventional bars for use on low-profile frames, as used in time trials and triathlons. Various degrees of drop, reach, width and shape are available, but the knees should always be behind the elbows. These bars are often used in conjunction with tri-bars.

Road-racing refinements

Careful bar choice can eradicate odd aches and pains. Most bikes come with handlebars of the 'standard' 42cm width, as measured from centre

LEFT: *With his elbows tucked in, a flat back and his head down, this triathlete is maintaining an excellent position. Note that in order to do this he has to sit far forward on the saddle.*
TOP: *Special dedicated unit aerobars offer significant weight savings over standard aero bar/lo-profile bar combinations*
ABOVE *Cinelli Spinaci clip-on bars are not legal for road racing.*
RIGHT: *The Look Ergo stem allows a wide range of positions to be tried. It is expensive, but a good investment for a club.*
TOP RIGHT: *Once you have the position broadly right, perfect it with the help of a friend or using a mirror.*

∙∙

to centre of the bar ends. Widths of 38–46cm are available, but some are measured from their outside edges. The bars should be the same width as the rider's shoulders, to make bike

control and breathing as efficient as possible. Drop depth, reach and degree of curve at the handlebar shoulders also vary. 'Anatomic' bars have a flattened forward drop, but they

increase the brake-lever reach. Most high-quality bars have either a brake-cable channel or brake- and gear-cable channels for Campagnolo Ergopower dual shifters, so that the cables do not protrude under the bar tape.

Aluminium has long been the prime choice of material for handlebars, but

carbon fibre bars are becoming more and more popular, as they are both lightweight and stiff. But remember that they can be very expensive, and should be replaced after a hard crash.

Handlebar stems

First and foremost your handlebar stem should be of a material which is compatible to your choice of bars – if possible try not to mix carbon and aluminium. Secondly look for rigidity, especially if you're a heavy rider, need a longer stem, or intend adding tri bars.

Most stems are of the threadless kind these days, and many are made from welded titanium or chromoly, making them very rigid, as well as lightweight. Carbon stems are also quite rigid when used with carbon bars, but if you add tri bars be sure to avoid tightening them too much when you have carbon bars.

CHAPTER 7

Buying a bike – the components

Once you have found a suitable frame, your major buying considerations will be the various components, in particular the groupset and wheels. Many people buy their dream frame and then

cannot justify spending vast sums on building it up: a set of even the cheapest components can cost nearly as much as a complete entry-level bike. If you are buying a bike off the peg, you may have little choice about the components that come with it, but some dealers will build up your choice of frame and components, and some

offer special packages. This chapter is designed to help you as you replace worn components or upgrade; it covers both the function of the various components and the compatibility of different makes.

The groupset

The groupset is the collective name for the gearing, braking and bearing components of a bike. Some groupsets also include the pedals, seat post and handlebar stem. Each manufacturer produces a number of different groupsets, which vary in quality and function.

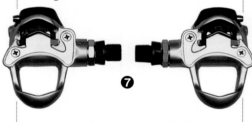

❺

Uniform styling in the components of a particular groupset helps make the bike look attractive. More importantly, components may function at their best only when used with others from the same groupset, or at least from the same manufacturer; this is particularly the case with Shimano groupsets.

❶

Campagnolo and Shimano are the best-known manufacturers of groupsets and are equally respected in the racing world. Mostly for reasons of cost, bike manufacturers may mix and match components from a given brand with those from smaller, independent companies. On entry-level bikes,

❷

❸

❹

cheap unbranded components – for example front hubs and chainsets – are often used.

Entry-level groupsets offer the basics you need to race, and are becoming increasingly sophisticated as features from the top end of the market trickle down.

Most come with lower gearing than those further up the range, and with the option of a triple chainset. If you are just starting out, such features may be more suitable for you than those of the higher-end groupsets. For many riders, mid-range groupsets, with more options and a higher bearing quality, offer the best compromise between performance and price. Again, a triple chainset is usually an option.

❻

Shimano Dura-Ace and Campagnolo Record are the 'flagship' groupsets on which all new developments are first seen: for instance, both now offer ten-speed systems. Increasingly, to save weight, their components are made from titanium and carbon fibre and manufactured using specialist

techniques. Hollow cranks are now commonplace, as are titanium and carbon fibre bolts and sections. While the high end models are considerably more expensive than other models, they are also the most reliable and longest lasting: many of the component parts are made by forging, an expensive process that re-aligns the grain of the metal to give strength where it is needed most.

❼

Bearings and pivots are of the highest quality, for minimal friction and maximum life. Another advantage is that spare parts are more readily available than for cheaper groupsets; these are often also

❽

compatible with the same manufacturer's lower-end groupsets.

'After-market' components

What have become known as 'after-market' components are sold by some independent manufacturers to take

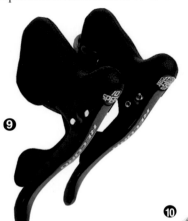

❾

the place of those supplied with off-the-peg bikes or as part of a groupset. Such components are often fitted to new bikes. Typical products are hubs, cassette cogs, chainsets, bottom brackets, chains and headsets. As the producers cannot

❿

⓫ compete in volume, they often specialise, aiming to fill gaps in the larger manufacturers' ranges; in the worst cases, they offer novelty value only. After-market components do help to break the somewhat artificial groupset concept: the greater the

⓬

interchangeability between components, the more competition, and the less restricted you are in modifying your bike.

The fixed gear

A fixed-gear arrangement is used for all track racing and by a few cyclists for training. A special hub is required, with a single 'fixed' cog and no freewheel. The pedals feel directly linked to the wheel, offering great response and control. On the track, no brakes are required (or in fact allowed), as the bike can be slowed by exerting backward pressure on the pedals; for road use, a front brake is a legal

The fixed gear is the simplest, lightest and most elegant means of transmission for a bicycle.

requirement in the UK, the USA and most European countries. Campagnolo, Shimano and the lesser-known and less expensive manufacturer Miche all make these specialist track components.

THE CAMPAGNOLO RECORD GROUPSET

1 Front hub
2 Bottom-bracket cartridge
3 Rear hub (free hub)
4 Cassette
5 Chainset
6 Front derailleur
7 Clipless pedals
8 Seat post
9 Dual brake lever and gear shifter
10 Rear derailleur
11 Headset
12 Chain
13 Dual pivot brake

⓭

The gearing system

If you understand what each component does, you will find buying replacements or upgrades much easier, and troubleshooting will be quicker, too. Components from different manufacturers and groupsets may not be compatible, so choose with care.

Shimano STI and Campagnolo Ergopower dual gear and brake shifters are now the norm on all but some entry-level bikes. Because they allow you to brake, change gear and steer without altering the position of your hands on the bars, you can maintain a regular pedalling cadence. With down-tube gear shifters, not only do you lose momentum and concentration while you reach down, but you also signal to your rivals that you may be about to attack.

When you change gear, the gear-shift levers increase or reduce the tension of the gear cables by precise amounts, moving the derailleur to match the spacing between the cassette cogs or the chainrings. This is known as indexing.

Good-quality gear cables, which are often made of stainless steel, are designed not to stretch, so as to keep these movements precise. Similarly, the gear cable housing is designed not to compress or to restrict the movement of the cable in any other way: it has an inner nylon or Teflon core for smoothness. End caps are fitted to ensure that the cable sits in a precise position and to reinforce its end. Some end caps have seals to help prevent water entering the housing and corroding the cable.

There are normally two cable adjusters, one on the down tube and one on the rear derailleur: unscrewing them shortens the cable, and vice

The gearing system components

Gear cable housing

Cassette

Gear shifters

Down tube cable adjuster

Gear cable

Front derailleur

Chainset

Chain

Rear hub (free hub)

Rear derailleur

Rear derailleur adjuster

versa. This means that it is possible to set the precise tension of the cable in order to line up each gear click with an individual cog or chainring. The down-tube adjuster, used with handlebar-mounted gear shifters, allows fine adjustments to be made whilst racing. The adjuster on the rear derailleur is normally used in the workshop (see pages 154–5).

Derailleurs

The action of shifting down into a larger rear cog causes the cable to pull the rear derailleur across, acting against its spring; as you shift up into a smaller cog, the gear-shift lever and cable determine how far the derailleur spring returns. It is therefore important to use a rear derailleur and a gear shifter that are designed for use together; otherwise, the cable movements may be too large or small. See the table below for details of

which shifter is compatible with what derailleur.

Each model has a maximum rear cog size and a gear capacity rating (the maximum difference between the smallest cog and largest chainring that it can handle while keeping the chain properly tensioned). The upper pulley of all Shimano and some other derailleurs has a little lateral play, or 'float', so that it can align itself with the cog, giving smoother changes and less noise.

The design of the front derailleur is much less critical than that of the rear. It will have a maximum recommended chainring size, and its rated capacity is the difference in the number of teeth between the larger and smaller chainring.

Rear hub (free hub)

Hubs are normally 130mm across the locknuts for eight, nine or ten-speed. Cassette bodies are designed for either Shimano or Campagnolo cassettes and for either eight, nine or ten sprockets.

Campagnolo and Shimano hubs contain conventional ball bearings, of a 'cup and cone' design. These need regular lubrication and adjustment. A number of high-quality hubs have

Both Shimano and Campagnolo use a spider system for the larger rear sprockets in order to save weight. Titanium saves even more weight on the most expensive cassettes.

sealed cartridge bearings, where the ball bearings are contained within a special housing.

Chains

You will find that you can achieve the smoothest gear shifts by using the cassette manufacturer's recommended chain and chain length. Special ultra-narrow chains are used on nine- and ten-speed cassettes. Almost all modern chainrings and cassette cogs have various ramps, gates and pins to help the chain shift.

Gear ratios

A gear ratio is a figure that enables you to calculate the combined effect of a given cassette cog, chainring and wheel size. It tells you objectively how easy or hard a given gear is and helps you to find new combinations if those you have are not suitable.

In English-speaking countries, gear ratios are calculated as the equivalent wheel diameter of a direct-drive bike, in inches (see diagram below and box opposite). (This is a hangover from the days of high-wheel bicycles or 'penny farthings'.)

In continental Europe, gear ratios are expressed as the development. This is the distance travelled forward for one revolution of the pedals, in metres (see box opposite).

Remember that tyre size affects the wheel diameter, so for total accuracy this should be measured exactly from tread to tread.

Either system is effective as a means of comparison: the higher the figure, the harder you push or the more slowly you pedal. To avoid confusion, cyclists often refer to ratios as simply 52 x 14, 42 x 21 and so on.

A suitable range of gears

As you ride, you may find that you do not have a gear high enough to enable you to go as fast as you want on the flat or downhill, or that when climbing steep hills you stall and exhaust yourself. You may also need a bail-out gear for getting home if you 'blow up'. Similarly, if you find that a frequently used gear feels too high, but the next is too low, you may want to fit a sprocket of intermediate size.

With modern cassettes particularly those with spiders, such as the latest nine and ten speed ones, it's not possible to mix and match sprockets. You have to use one of the standard cassette ratios. It is worthwhile though to study the cassettes which are available and see which will suit your needs better. With nine and ten speeds available you should be able to have a gear for any situation.

Avoid using the smallest chainring with the smallest rear cog or the biggest chainring with the biggest rear cog, as this is inefficient and causes rapid wear to the system because of the extreme chain angle.

The table below shows suitable gears for various riding requirements.

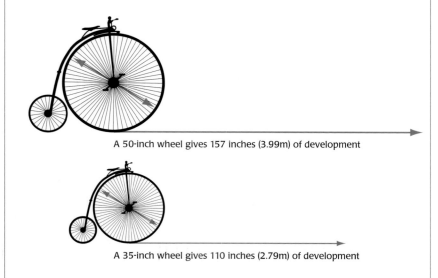

A 50-inch wheel gives 157 inches (3.99m) of development

A 35-inch wheel gives 110 inches (2.79m) of development

The larger the wheel, the further it travels for one revolution of the pedals. Similarly, the larger the gear, the further you will travel for one pedal revolution. The gear ratio in inches (the English system) tells you how big a wheel you would have to use on a direct-drive bike to achieve the same 'development' (the distance travelled for one revolution) as in a given gear.

Gear size (inches)	Use
< 40	Mountain and touring bikes
41–50	Hill climbing
51–60	Lowest gears for flattish courses
61–70	Lowest gears for flat time trials
71–100	Normal gears
>100	Flat-out gears

ABOVE: *Knowing your gears and selecting the right combination is vital.*

A gear ratio in inches is calculated like this:

$$\frac{\text{chainring size (no. of teeth)}}{\text{cassette cog size (no. of teeth)}} \times \text{wheel diameter (inches) measured tread to tread}$$

For example: $\dfrac{52}{14} \times 26.4$ inches (typical 700C wheel) = 98 inches

Development (in metres) is calculated like this:

$$\frac{\text{chainring size (no. of teeth)}}{\text{cassette cog size (no. of teeth)}} \times \text{wheel diameter (metres)} \times \pi\ (3.14)$$

For example: $\dfrac{52}{14} \times 0.67$m (typical 700C wheel) x 3.14 = 7.81m

---

The following tables show appropriate ranges of gear ratios, based on 700C wheels and a nominal 26.4in wheel diameter, for various types of racing. The figures across the top of each table are the number of teeth on the rear sprockets, and the figures in the left-hand column are the number of teeth on the chainrings. The gear ratios themselves are expressed in inches.

	12	13	14	15	16	17	19	21
52	114	106	98	92	86	81	72	-
42	-	85	79	74	69	65	58	53

ROAD RACING – EIGHT SPEED For a fit cyclist, these ratios give a reasonable range, and the gaps between them are not too big.

	12	13	14	15	17	19	21	23	25
53	117	108	100	93	82	74	67	61	-
42	-	85	79	74	65	58	53	48	44

ROAD RACING – NINE SPEED It's possible to get both bigger gears and smaller gears without increasing the gaps between the gears. This is an advantage when racing in hilly areas.

	12	13	14	15	16	17	18	19	21
53	117	108	100	93	87	82	78	74	-
42	-	85	79	74	69	65	62	58	53

TIME TRIALLING In Time trialling keeping a very even cadence is desirable in order to maximise your effort evenly over the whole course. Smaller gaps between the gears will help you to maintain your pedalling cadence at around 85–100rpm. Nine and ten speed cassettes still give you a suitably low gear for any climbs.

	12	13	14	15	17	19	21	23
52	114	106	98	92	81	72	65	-
39	-	79	74	69	61	54	49	45

HILLY COURSES/BEGINNERS/TRAINING The smallest ring that may normally be fitted to a road-racing chainset is one with 39 teeth. Its use is generally to be avoided, as shifts to the smaller ring are too great, resulting in a sudden loss of momentum and/or double gear shifts.

The chainset and bottom bracket

Your efforts are transmitted through the chainset and bottom bracket, which means that this is a very important area of the bike. Although it is possible to upgrade both components, many of the items on the market offer few advantages, so choose with care.

The chainset is made up of two cranks, with one, two or three chainrings bolted to the 'spider' that forms part of the right-hand crank. The chainrings are detachable on all but the cheapest models, so that gear ratios can be altered easily. The number of teeth you can use is determined by the capacity of your gear mechanisms, but when buying replacements you must also know the bolt-circle diameter (BCD) of your crank (see below). Most road chainsets have a 130mm BCD, except those made by Campagnolo, whose BCD is 135mm.

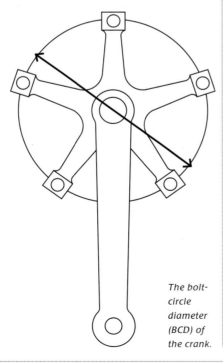

The bolt-circle diameter (BCD) of the crank.

Triple chainsets are rarely used by racers, but less fit riders, those living in hilly areas and Audax/randonneur cyclists often benefit from them. Most road chainsets are designed as doubles, but special inner chainrings are available from TA: this allows a third ring, down to 24 teeth, to be fitted inexpensively.

Many independent manufacturers, such as Truvativ and FSA, now produce great crank sets and chainrings, in various materials, which are compatible with the major systems and are often a little cheaper – and are definitely more fashionable.

Crank length

Most cranks are available only in 170 and 175mm lengths. These are fine if your inside-leg measurement is on the long side of 'average', but otherwise they can seriously reduce your pedalling efficiency.

Cranks that are too short do not allow the full leverage of the legs to be used; those that are too long force the knee, hip, and ankle to bend more than necessary, often resulting in a slow cadence and a greater risk of knee injury. You need to reach a compromise to suit your own leg length.

Alternative crank lengths are sometimes available in the higher-end Shimano groupsets and from some smaller manufacturers. If you have the funds to experiment, you could start with cranks that are 20–21 per cent of your inside-leg measurement. (Since shorter cranks are not always available, you may have to settle for something a little longer than ideal.) Bear in mind that a change of crank

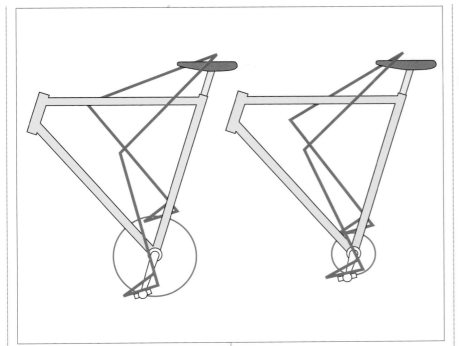

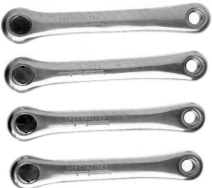

LEFT: *Cranks that are too long cramp the knee, hip and ankle.* RIGHT: *cranks that are too short reduce leverage.*

Only TA, the specialist French manufacturer, makes cranks in lengths less than 165mm and greater than 180mm. The full range covers 150–185mm in 2.5mm increments.

length may necessitate a change of saddle height, and that it will also affect your gear ratios: because of the reduced pedalling force, shorter cranks require lower ratios, and vice versa. As a guide, you can expect to use gear ratios five inches lower (higher) for every 5mm the crank is shorter (longer) than 170mm. The

Inside-leg measurement (cm)	Crank length (mm)
72–75	155–160
76–79	160–165
80–83	165–170
84–87	170–175
88–91	175–180
92–95	180–185

table below gives the recommended crank lengths.

One potential advantage of using the correct length of crank is that if you have a custom frame built, the builder may be able to make beneficial adjustments to the frame geometry. Better handling, a lower or higher bottom bracket, the prevention of interference with the front wheel by the toe and/or a shorter top tube are all benefits it may be possible to achieve.

For reasons of fashion and habit, many cyclists use cranks that are too long for them. In particular, you may notice that professional racers sometimes use longer cranks than appears necessary. There are many myths surrounding crank length, and the pros are just as susceptible to them as any other cyclist.

Bottom-bracket bearings

Almost all bottom-bracket bearing units are now cartridge units; the bearings and axle are contained in a single unit held in the frame by retaining cups. These require minimal maintenance and generally last two to three years. More expensive models tend to be smoother, better sealed, more reliable and lighter – titanium axles are common on the most up-market models. Many of these have replaceable bearing units that cost about the same as a cheap cartridge unit. When you do need to replace a bottom bracket be sure to be armed with not only the exact model details, but also details of your frame, as threads can differ at times.

Traditional units are rarely used on new bikes. These consist of a separate axle, cups and ball bearings. They require regular adjustment checks and a yearly overhaul.

Pedals

Most of your effort goes through the pedals, so efficiency and comfort are vital. Clipless pedal systems are the best solution, as they hold and support the foot well, and release the shoe more quickly and reliably than clipped pedals. Because there are several pedal systems, most bikes are sold with no pedals, or with extremely cheap ones.

Shoe cleats, whether clipless or with the traditional toe-clips, are designed to keep your foot from moving on the pedal, as this only wastes energy and distracts you. The cleats should align the foot perpendicularly across the pedal axis to reduce the risk of knee problems such as tendinitis. Most systems allow for some rotational movement of the shoe whilst riding: this is known as 'float', and does not normally interfere with pedalling.

No-float systems or settings are the most positive, but require much more careful setting up. Some riders position their shoes so that the toes point in or out a little. This may be necessary to avoid the heel or ankle knocking the crank or to prevent knee or foot pain: never force your feet to point straight ahead if it is uncomfortable.

You should pedal with the ball of your foot centred over the pedal spindle for maximum efficiency.

Having the foot too far forward feels more powerful, but it allows less ankle movement, and this reduces efficiency. A slightly forward position can suit riders who pedal slowly, those with large feet and those who suffer from sore calf muscles or Achilles tendons. With the foot too far back, the pedal stroke becomes very supple, but there is a marked reduction in power. Positioning the foot slightly to the rear can suit riders who pedal at high cadences and those with small feet.

A properly set-up pedal and shoe arrangement gives you the confidence to pedal positively.

Look system pedal and cleat.

Setting shoe cleats

Cleats must be properly fitted and tightened before being ridden; otherwise, you may be unable to release your feet. Grease the bolts, fit the cleats approximately straight on the shoes, and tighten firm. Set both pedals' cleat-retention systems at their lowest tension (on some models only — see below). Support yourself against a wall, back pedal and judge your foot position: you will probably want to readjust the cleats. Different pedals and shoes may be of differing heights so require a small adjustment to saddle height.

Practise engaging and removing both feet until you feel comfortable with the system. Then find a straight, flat bit of road where you can experiment and build up your confidence. Further adjustment may be necessary: ideally, the cleats should allow equal float in both directions, so that the foot is not hindered in finding its natural position. Finally, ensure the cleats are fully tightened and adjust the pedal tension to produce as positive an action as you require.

The pedal systems

The first clipless pedal system was designed by French ski binding manufacturer Look, and their system is still popular today. The basic principle in most systems is based around a spring-loaded pedal and a cleat. To clip in you push the front of the cleat into the pedal and push down to allow the rear to 'spring' into the pedal trap. To release, most systems work on an outward twist of the ankle. It can take a while to get used to, but it eventually becomes second nature.

There are various pedal and cleat systems on the market. Most offer adjustable float and release tension, while some offer no-float options too. When buying shoes and pedals it is important to check cleat compatibility; many touring/mountain-bike-style shoes will only accept smaller SPD style cleats, while most road-specific shoes will not accept the smaller cleats.

Shimano SPD-R system pedal and cleat.

Time Pro system pedal and cleat.

Campagnolo Pro-Fit system pedal and cleat.

The braking system

The braking system is made up of the brake callipers, the brake blocks, the cables and cable housing, the control levers and the wheel rims (effectively the brake 'disc'). All play an important part in the power and modulation of the brake.

Shimano and Campagnolo dual-pivot callipers are now by far the most commonly used type of brake. The design is very similar throughout the groupsets, and all offer plenty of power though some riders complain that the modulation (the term used to describe degree of control) is not as good.

Single-pivot brakes are now not found on new road bikes although they are often found on older bikes. They are not as powerful and are trickier to set up.

When you are buying brakes, you should take into account the brake's drop (or reach), to ensure that the

Calliper brakes would become hopelessly clogged in the muddy conditions common in cyclo-cross. Instead, wide-profile cantilevers are used.

brake blocks will line up with the rim. Brake drop is measured from the centre of the brake mounting point to the centre of the rim's braking surface. Road-racing frames are designed to accommodate a brake drop of between 39 and 47mm.

Brake blocks and cables

Brake blocks vary greatly in their effectiveness in wet and dry conditions (in terms of both power and modulation), their lifespan, their proneness to noise and squeal, and their tendency to collect grit. It is worth finding a type you like and knowing its characteristics.

Better-quality cable housing has a nylon or Teflon liner to increase the smoothness of operation and the modulation, and to reduce the effort that is needed to apply the brakes.

Cantilever systems

These are an essential requirement for cyclo-cross bikes, in order to achieve the necessary clearance and power. However, because they are now almost wholly designed for mountain

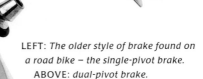

LEFT: The older style of brake found on a road bike – the single-pivot brake. ABOVE: dual-pivot brake.

bikes, modern cantilevers are less suited to drop-handlebar brake levers, which have too much leverage for them. This means that even with the brake blocks positioned right next to the rims, the brakes feel very 'spongy', and run the risk of not being powerful enough. The solution is to use either a special cyclo-cross brake lever (the hard-to-find Dia Compe 287S) or a pair of older, wide-profile cantilevers.

V-style brakes which fit onto the same braze-on fittings as cantilevers can also be fitted to cyclo-cross bikes. The same problems but even more so apply to using standard road bike brake levers with them. The answer comes in the form of a V-brake adaptor, of which there are several types available. This reduces the effective leverage of the V-style brake itself.

The headset

The purpose of the headset is to keep the forks attached to the frame. It must allow the forks to turn smoothly and freely, with no hint of sticking or binding or any trace of play. Any such problems will seriously – and dangerously – affect the bike's handling.

Mountain-bike Aheadset components are found on some racing bikes.

For decades the same threaded headset system, with a locking top nut, was used in conjunction with a wedge-style fastening stem, and some older bikes and lower-end bikes still use it. Now, however, nearly all bikes come with the threadless 'Aheadset' design as standard.

The threadless system is a lot lighter, more rigid, and easier to fit and maintain than its predecessor. But one shortfall of the system is its inherent lack of adjustability. The only options for bar height adjustment lie in using spacers, or turning the stem upside down, so it is important to make sure that the forks on a new bike have not been cut off too short, or you lose that adjustment option.

Many manufacturers now use 'integrated' threadless systems, which are very neat-looking and also very efficient. These systems have oversized top and bottom head tubes on the frame, and the headset is neatly housed inside the frame itself.

If you have an old-style wedge system it is possible to convert it to threadless by buying new threadless forks, headset and stem. If the frame is of sufficient quality this could be worth considering, as quality wedge stems

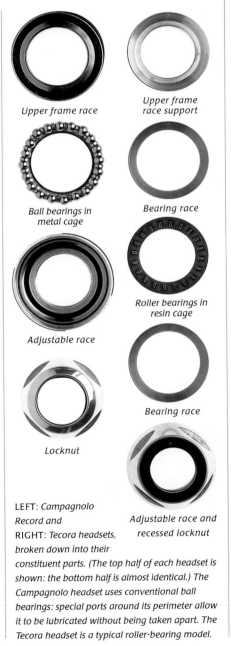

Upper frame race

Upper frame race support

Ball bearings in metal cage

Bearing race

Adjustable race

Roller bearings in resin cage

Locknut

Bearing race

Adjustable race and recessed locknut

LEFT: *Campagnolo Record and* RIGHT: *Tecora headsets, broken down into their constituent parts. (The top half of each headset is shown: the bottom half is almost identical.) The Campagnolo headset uses conventional ball bearings: special ports around its perimeter allow it to be lubricated without being taken apart. The Tecora headset is a typical roller-bearing model.*

and headsets are rapidly disappearing from the shelves of bike shops.

Headsets have a hard life. Unlike the other bearings on your bike, these are loaded axially: when you go over a bump, the force goes straight up through the bearings. The lower set of bearings take most of the shock, and as they only move a very small amount, they tend to form indentations in the lower races. This effect is known as 'brinelling' and makes the forks impossible to move precisely, causing tricky handling.

Two main bearing designs are used on both the traditional and threadless designs. The majority utilise conventional ball bearings. Roller-bearing models resist brinelling much better, but they should be fitted by an expert with special tools, as they must be more precisely aligned. Such models usually have the advantage that the inner races can be replaced separately from the cups, making overhaul cheaper and easier. A sealed headset is a good idea, as a bike without mudguards throws water and dirt right up under the headset.

Tyres and tubes

Both wheels and tyres have a considerable effect on the feel of your bike and – crucially, perhaps – on your ability to accelerate. A good-quality, lightweight pair of tyres and tubes will reduce rolling resistance, improve handling, grip and comfort, and help prevent punctures: they are one of the best, and cheapest, investments you can make.

Tyres (together with the rims they sit on) fall into two broad categories: tubular and wired-on. Almost all new road bikes now come with wired-on tyres as standard. These have a U-shaped cross-section and a wire or Kevlar bead running around their edges to hold the tyre against the edges of the rim, which are slightly hooked inwards. Wired-on tyres use a separate inner tube.

Tubular tyres, also known as tubs and sew-ups, are the traditional racing tyre. As their name suggests, they resemble a circular tube; they also have a special sewn-in inner tube, normally of latex. Tubulars are usually very light and are glued onto special lightweight 'sprint' rims of a suitable width. Good tubulars are also more comfortable than wired-on tyres, corner better and are less susceptible to pinch punctures. The very best have the minimum of rolling resistance. The disadvantage is that they are expensive and puncture repair is very tedious (as the tyre has to be unstitched and sewn up again), though temporary tyre replacement is quick. The continued development of high-performance wired-on tyres has made tubulars less attractive to all but the most keen riders, though they are still the norm on the track.

What to look for

A Kevlar bead, instead of wire, makes a tyre foldable, so that it can be carried as a spare, and saves a little weight, but it adds to the cost. A Kevlar belt protects against punctures, but it slightly increases the weight and rolling resistance, so is unsuitable for racing but useful for training.

All types of tyre can vary enormously in their vulnerability to cuts and punctures: if problems plague you, try another make. Some of the hardest-wearing tyres occasionally tend to cut more easily, as the rubber is less 'stretchy'. Thinner or finer-threaded casings are more supple and lighter, and offer reduced rolling resistance, improved cornering and grip and greater comfort.

The narrower a tyre is, the lighter and more aerodynamic it will be, but it will also be less comfortable because of its smaller air pocket. Tyre size has no significant effect on rolling resistance; the main way of reducing this is by increasing tyre pressure. Unlike car tyres, road-bike tyres do not need tread, as the narrow profile displaces water; tread serves only to decrease the area of contact with the road! Soft tread compounds tend to

LEFT: *The Continental Grand Prix is a popular tyre for time trials and road racing.*
CENTRE: *A tyre developed for track use.*
RIGHT: *A training tyre.*

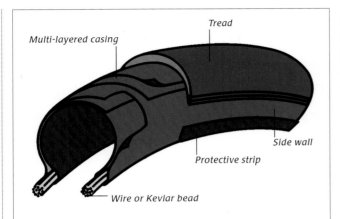

Multi-layered casing
Tread
Side wall
Protective strip
Wire or Kevlar bead

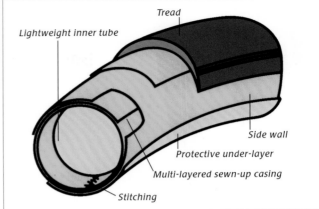

Tread
Lightweight inner tube
Side wall
Protective under-layer
Multi-layered sewn-up casing
Stitching

give the best grip, but a reduced wear life, so some tyre manufacturers compromise by using soft rubber towards the sides for cornering and a harder centre strip.

Some tyres have a raised central strip, which is claimed to reduce rolling resistance and increase tyre life, but these are not recommended as they can make cornering feel less certain.

It is a good idea to try out as many different types of tyre as possible: comfort, cornering, grip in wet and dry conditions and the feel of the handling can differ significantly, and individual riders' preferences also tend to vary.

A latex tube.

Tubes

Most tubes are made from butyl or the more expensive latex. Owing to its greater flexibility, latex reduces rolling resistance, but it loses pressure by about one bar (15psi) every eight hours. This could be a problem during a long race or endurance event. Mixed butyl/latex tubes such as AirB are a good compromise. Continental and Michelin tubes are also recommended. Polyurethane tubes are light but increase rolling resistance; they must be of precisely the correct size, as they do not stretch at all. Far Eastern tubes tend to be heavier and less supple than European ones.

The tube diameter must be matched to that of the tyre. If the tube

A long-valve tube.

LEFT: *A wired-on tyre is made up of a multi-layered casing, a tread and a mounting 'bead'.* RIGHT: *A tubular tyre has a sewn-up case enveloping a very light inner tube.*

....

is too narrow, it will be overstretched and may puncture; if it is too wide, it will be easy to trap it under the tyre bead, causing the tyre to blow off, and you will also be carrying surplus weight. Special tubes with a long valve extension are made for deep-section rims, or alternatively valve extenders may be used.

Rim tape

Protective rim tape is required before a wired-on tyre can be fitted to a rim. This prevents the sharp, irregular edges of the spoke holes and nipples from puncturing the tube. The rim tape must fit tightly and cover the full width of the rim. If you have Mavic rims, the yellow plastic rim tape sold specifically for them is recommended. Otherwise, use a rubber or sticky cloth tape. If a tyre is a loose fit, or you have trouble centring it, a double layer of tape, or a thicker one, may help. If the tyre is very tight, you could try using a thinner rim tape.

Rims

Rim quality varies considerably. Generally, lightness is the chief consideration, but this must not be achieved at the expense of strength. Deep aero-section rims often put aerodynamics before weight-saving. Poor rims tend to go out of true more easily and are harder to re-true.

A wide range of rims is available to suit almost any need.

Most rims for wired-on tyres are made from a box-section aluminium alloy extrusion (formed by forcing a hot aluminium tube through a shaping die), with internal bracing to make them stiffer and stronger. Wider and deeper rims are generally stiffer but heavier, and require less frequent truing.

Most rims are anodised, often grey, brown or black. This makes the rims resistant to corrosion, but wet-weather braking is impaired until the anodising is worn. Some rims have a machined braking surface, with any irregularities smoothed out and the unwanted section of anodising removed, and these give the best braking. Hard anodising can make rims stiffer but more vulnerable to cracking. Ceramic-coated rims are very expensive and may not be good for braking in dry weather, but they reduce brake wear and give better wet-weather braking, so may be useful for cyclo-cross. Carbon-fibre rims have a poor braking surface that wears quickly, limiting their use to flattish courses.

Most traditional-style rims are built for 32 spokes, but 36 spokes are used for the heaviest and hardest riding. Sometimes 28 spokes are used for time trialling, but deep aero-section rims commonly have far fewer. Eyelets are usually used to spread the stresses of spoke tension: double eyelets spread the stresses more widely, utilising the bracing part of the rim. Many aero rims use increased rim wall thickness instead of eyeletting.

Wheel size

The vast majority of racing bikes are fitted with 700C wheels. The tread-to-tread diameter of these is approximately 700mm, depending on the type used. The 'C' distinguishes these wheels from two other varieties of 700mm diameter wheel, used on utility bikes.

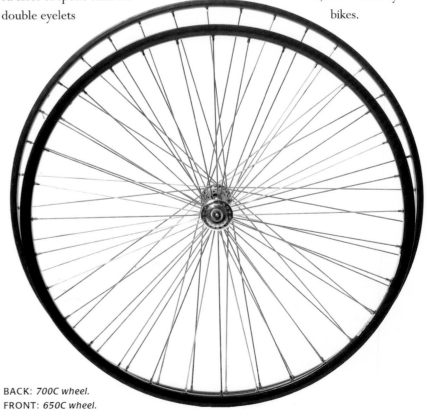

BACK: *700C wheel.*
FRONT: *650C wheel.*

LEFT: *A sprint rim for use with tubular tyres*
RIGHT: *A rim designed for wired-on tyres.*

You may find that 650C wheels are fitted to some triathlon and time-trial bikes. Historically, these wheels measured approximately 26 inches (650mm) from tread to tread, but for racing they are now just over an inch smaller; however, they are still often referred to as 26-inch wheels. Their main advantage is that they accelerate more quickly and help produce more agile handling. These wheels are not commonplace, so choice is limited, spares are hard to come by, and their use is consequently generally limited to special time trials.

Tyre and rim compatibility

Tyres that are too small in section for the rim will have an air pocket that has a flattened profile. This gives a harder ride and increases the likelihood of pinch punctures (where the tyre is squashed flat against the rim by a bump in the road). Too wide a tyre for the rim makes the tyre side walls more vulnerable to damage and can make cornering less certain. The table below shows the recommended tyres for various rim widths.

Tyre manufacturers use a number of different sizing systems. The ISO system is the only one consistently used internationally. The first figure denotes the tyre section and the second the diameter of the tyre's mounting bead and the rim's bead seat (the part of the rim where the tyre's bead sits). These figures are given in millimetres. The bead seat of 700C rims is 622mm and that of 650C rims is 571mm.

Wheel 'dish'

Cassette and multiple-cog free hubs have their spoke flanges offset to allow space for the cogs. To overcome this, the wheel is dished (see diagram below). However, this reduces the strength of the wheel, the more so for eight- and nine-speed hubs, which require more dish than seven-speed.

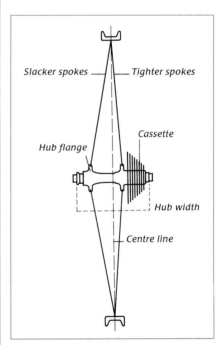

The spokes on the right-hand side are tighter than those on the left to centralise the rim between the locknuts of the hub.

RIM WIDTH (inside flanges)	TYRE SECTION (recommended)	TYPICAL USE
12–13mm	18–23mm	Time trialling, road racing
14–17mm	23–28mm	Road racing, long-distance time trials, training
18–20mm	28–37mm	Training, Audax/*randonnée*, touring

TYRE SIZE: Look for the tyre's ISO marking to determine its size.

Spoked wheels

Despite modern advances in wheel design, the spoked wheel still has a very important part to play, particularly in road racing, long-distance events and riding done on poor road surfaces, because of its comfort. Even the best spoked wheels are very cheap compared to the more exotic alternatives available.

A well-built spoked wheel is one of humankind's most efficient structures, in terms of its strength-to-weight ratio. The separate elements of rim, spokes and hub must each be chosen for the intended use.

Wheels are laced and trued by a machine and/or a skilled mechanic. The correct spoke tension is vital, and needs to be consistent. Wheels that are built with too much spoke tension will go wildly out of true if a spoke breaks; the spoke nipples will be hard to turn and may deform when the wheel is trued, and the hub flanges may crack. Spokes that are too loose will allow the rim to rub the brake, particularly when sprinting. The spoke nipples are also liable to undo through the cyclic stress on the spokes.

A competent wheel builder can ensure the maximum strength and reliability by carefully tensioning and 'bedding down' the spokes. Such wheels stay in true much longer, and any subsequent truing is usually easier. The spoke tension of an individually built wheel can be tailor-made for the rider and event: a very tight wheel with the minimum of flex might be used for track racing, a less highly tensioned wheel to ensure comfort on cobbled roads in classics such as Paris–Roubaix. In both cases, long-term reliability may be sacrificed for the possible gains in a single race.

Radially spoked wheels

If these wheels are built using conventional components, as on some time-trial and track bikes, they generally present more problems than advantages. Weight-saving and aerodynamic gains are very small and flanges of even top quality hubs frequently crack under the extra stresses imposed by radial spoking. Radial spoking is occasionally used for the left-hand side of rear wheels and is equally unwise. The only exceptions to this are the special factory built wheels where all the components have been designed specifically for radial spoking.

Factory wheels

Several manufacturers now offer complete factory-built spoked wheels. These frequently have fewer spokes and are high-tension built. They are often supplied with new bikes, and are generally good value and reliable. But they will always require their own special spokes and tensioning tools, so are best repaired by experienced mechanics.

On the rough cobbles of classics such as Paris–Roubaix and the Tour of Flanders, all the riders use spoked wheels for comfort.

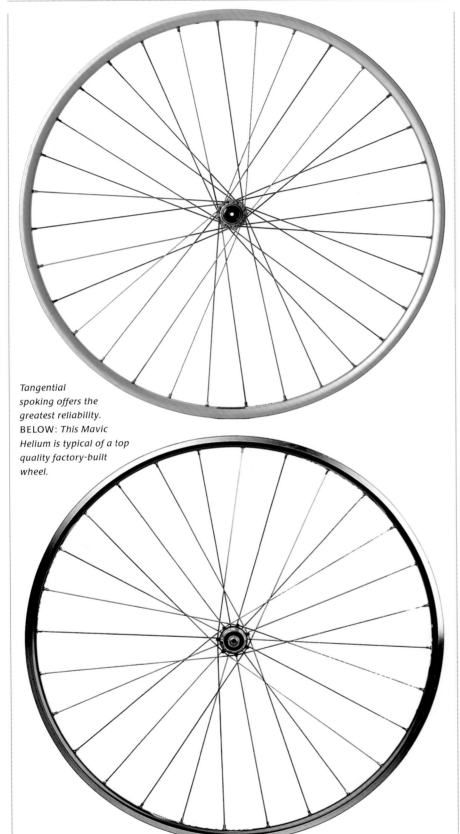

Tangential spoking offers the greatest reliability.
BELOW: *This Mavic Helium is typical of a top quality factory-built wheel.*

Spoke types

All modern racing spokes are made from stainless steel. Plain-gauge spokes, used on many entry-level bikes, are the same thickness throughout, but this does not give any extra strength. Double-butted spokes, used for most racing wheels, are

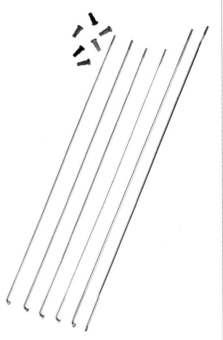

thinner in their middle section in order to save weight; most importantly, they also make for more reliable wheels, as their 'stretchiness' means they can be tightened further and more evenly than usual. Always try to choose a reputable brand such as DT Swiss or Sapim.

Bladed spokes have a flattened, lenticular shape. Though heavier, these reduce wind turbulence. They are usually used with special hubs and deep aero-section rim. Some have heads which enable them to be used with conventional hubs. Elliptical spokes have less aerodynamic advantages, but are lighter than bladed ones and fit most hubs.

Aero wheels

The faster you ride, the more difference air resistance makes: even quite small aerodynamic improvements can save vital seconds in a time trial. After tri-bars, aero wheels are your next major consideration, but they are a big investment.

Wheels must fight both forward air resistance and side winds, and also the churning effect of the spinning spokes. The purpose of aero wheels is to minimise all these factors. While such wheels will be of most use to time triallists and triathletes, road racers may also benefit.

Not all aero wheels are as stiff as conventionally spoked wheels, and so they may adversely affect the bike's handling. Most are a little heavier, meaning that you need more energy to accelerate; this is an important consideration for courses with lots of corners and climbs. Some 'aero' wheels can in fact create greater wind resistance in side winds than conventional wheels, and this may make the bike difficult to control. An aero wheel at the front is generally of more help than at the rear; if you do use a rear wheel, make sure the hub is compatible with your gearing system. (See pages 110–11.)

Deep aero-section wheels

Nowadays, these are almost *de rigueur* in time trials and triathlons, owing to their good aerodynamic characteristics, reasonable immunity to side winds and moderate cost. The less extreme versions are also increasingly being used in road racing, particularly in short, flat events where their much reduced shock absorbency is less critical. If you find yourself in a lone breakaway, these wheels could make the difference between winning and getting caught by the bunch. In short, they are the best compromise purchase for a mixture of road-race and time-trial use.

The rims come in two materials. Deep aluminium rims are very stiff and strong but somewhat heavy, though they have the advantage of needing as few as twelve spokes, which reduces weight and wind resistance. As they have a good braking surface, they may be used on hilly and tight courses, although they perform best overall on flattish terrain. Deep carbon-fibre rims are light, but have a poor, rapidly worn

LEFT: *Rolf Vector wheel with unusual new spoking pattern.* CENTRE: *Campagnolo Shamal aluminium alloy wheel.* RIGHT: *The Specialized wheel is a versatile, tried-and-tested design, with good overall performance, and is relatively comfortable to ride.*

braking surface. Combined carbon-fibre and aluminium rims can offer the advantages of lightness and stiffness, as well as good braking; an aluminium braking surface is also the norm on tri-spoke and disc wheels.

Radial spoking is commonly used, made possible by the use of specially designed hubs and spokes. In fact, so few spokes cannot easily be built into a tangential pattern.

Tri-spoke wheels

This term is generally used for three- and four-bladed wheels. These work in the same way as deep aero-section wheels but are more affected by side winds and are more expensive. The use of front tri-spoke wheels is not recommended in windy conditions. They are legal for road racing.

Disc wheels

These provide the least drag of all aero wheels; a lenticular shape has

A HED disc wheel.

The advantages of aero wheels can be accurately assessed in a wind tunnel.

been found to give the very best aerodynamic profile. Disc wheels are heavier and more susceptible to crosswinds than other aero wheels, which makes them suitable only for use on the rear. They are not legal in road races. Much cheaper, but hard to find, is a disc cover to fit a conventional wheel. These usually add minimal weight but do not affect wheel stiffness.

Wind-tunnel test results on some of the most popular styles of wheels. The figures show drag in pounds measured at 30mph (49km/h). A wind angle of zero degrees is a headwind. As you can see, performance varies greatly. The full disc wheel in a 15-degree side wind will start to act like a sail, providing a very small amount of forward thrust.

WHEEL MODEL	ANGLE OF WIND (°)				
	0	5	7.5	10	15
Standard 32-spoke wheel	0.50	0.65	0.49	0.49	0.53
Aluminium deep-section aero	0.44	0.42	0.44	0.46	0.46
Aluminium/carbon deep-section aero	0.48	0.46	0.48	0.44	0.46
Ultra deep section aero	0.32	0.29	0.27	0.27	0.21
Tri-spoke	0.38	0.38	0.37	0.34	0.21
Full rear disc	0.25	0.23	0.17	0.12	-0.01

Computers and accessories

Some carefully chosen accessories will make your cycling more convenient, comfortable and efficient.

A bike computer should monitor your current speed, your average speed, the distance covered and the time taken. With this information, you can assess your progress during a race, especially in a time trial, and modify it if necessary: if your legs are up to it, this may make all the difference between winning and being an 'also-

ran'. Computers are equally useful to assess and improve your training. Cordless computers are the neatest, but are by no means necessary. Most computers will display the maximum speed reached, but the cheapest show only the current speed to the nearest whole mile/kilometre per hour; the most expensive models can display trip altitude climbed and cadence. Adequate waterproofing can be an issue with some types. Additional fitting kits (mounting bracket, sensor and magnet) enable you to swap the computer easily between bikes, but you may need to recalibrate it for different tyres or wheel sizes. The latest cycle computers from Shimano (Flight Deck) and Campagnolo

(Ergobrain) are linked into the gearshifters and can according to the model, tell you your cadence and which gear you are pedalling, in addition to the usual functions.

Heart (pulse) monitors

Pulse monitors give a scientific measure of how hard you are working. All you really need to know is the pulse rate, but some models bleep if your rate moves beyond pre-set limits, tell you how much time you have spent within given zones, and record recovery rate; some also have a memory for later use. (See Chapter 5 for more about using heart-rate monitors.)

Some manufacturers offer great multifunction units that combine computers with HRMs, and some even with GPS systems, which provide details that you can download to your computer to give precise training and ride route logs and charts.

Many top professional riders now use SRM Power Cranks, or even Power Tap

Hubs, as a matter of course during their training. These enable them to combine accurate power Wattage ratings with heart rates to judge their training precisely. These systems are great for the ultra-serious, but are still very expensive, and beyond the reach of most riders.

Car racks

Car racks fall into four categories; roof, towbar mounted, towball mounted and strap-on.

Roof racks can carry bicycles right way up with wheels in, right way up with front wheel out and upside down. Those that hold the bike by the front fork and the rear wheel are far quicker and easier to use than the others. Up to four bikes can be carried depending on the car's width and its rated maximum roof load. Roof racks have some disadvantages: the bikes have to be lifted up to roof level and increase fuel consumption by 10-20%.

Towbar mounted racks have a fitting that sits between the towball and bar into which the rack fits. The best are the wheel support type which

....

TOP: *Power cranks are expensive, but are fast becoming a popular way to monitor training progress.*
ABOVE LEFT: *Computers take the guesswork out of assessing your pace.*
LEFT: *A heart-rate monitor is a good way of ensuring that the training you do is effective, and of spotting potential health and performance problems.*

1 High mount strap fitted rack.
2 Front wheel out style roof fittings.
3 Wheel support towbar mounted rack.
4 Standard two arm towbar mounted rack.

keep the bikes well apart from each other. The other, more common type of towbar rack uses two support arms to carry up to three bikes. They are a lot cheaper but harder on your bikes.

Tow ball mounted racks clamp around the towball and most are extremely easy to fit. Two protruding arms generally carry the bikes.

Strap-on racks strap on to the boot or rear door. They are losing favour for several reasons. They need a lot of care in fitting in order to be truly secure and are not very kind to your bikes unless extra padding is used. Strap mounted racks are best used for fairly short journeys. Rack stability is all important; the best strap-on racks have six straps. There are several strap mount racks available that lift the bikes clear of the lights and number plate and this removes the necessity for electrics. All others will need towbar electrics and a lighting board on most

RIGHT: *The Cool Tool will solve most on-the-road problems, yet takes up little more room than a small adjustable spanner.*
FAR RIGHT: *A saddle pack is virtually a necessity for training.*

cars. Finally there are strap-on wheel support racks that will generally carry two bikes. These look after your bikes far better than the standard type and do not need a lighting board.

Training bits and pieces

Multi-purpose 'road' tools, providing the essentials for adjustment or breakdown, are ideal for training rides. The Cool Tool and Ritchey models are some of the best.

Small clip-on saddle packs are very useful for carrying the essentials on a training ride. Some are expandable and large enough to take a compact waterproof jacket.

A frame pump is essential. Get a 'frame-fit' pump that sits parallel to the seat tube and is held in place by the top tube and down tube. Mini-pumps

will fit inside some saddle packs, but are usually quite inefficient.

For rides at dusk or dawn, you will need lights. LED rear lamps are compact and lightweight. However, as they are not always entirely visible from side angles, most models are not technically legal in the UK and some other countries. Requirements in the USA can vary from state to state.

Unless you know your LED light meets legal standards (consult your dealer for information), it is best used in conjunction with an approved rear light. Most racers prefer a compact halogen bulb front light. Many of these are heavy on battery usage, and so are best powered by rechargeable batteries. There are some excellent rechargeable systems available for regular night-time use from Vistalite and Cateye.

Clothing

Choosing and wearing the correct clothing for training and racing is absolutely essential for your health, performance and comfort. However, there are so many different fabrics and garments on sale, and so many claims

are made for them, that you become spoiled for choice, and buying what is right for you can be extremely difficult. All too often, even the best clothing is worn in the

wrong circumstances, or combined with other items in ways that make it ineffective. This chapter contains some good, practical advice on choosing and wearing appropriate types of clothing, shoes and helmets, as well as giving you some traditional 'tricks of the trade' that you might otherwise never discover.

Summer clothing

It is very tempting just to strip off to ride in the summer, but if you do you could be risking all sorts of infections and abrasions.

No matter how hot it is, you should always wear an undervest. This should be made from an ABL (action base layer) fibre that will 'wick away' the sweat from your body, leaving you dry and keeping colds at bay. Cotton t-shirts act as sponges, which means you will feel wet and cold when you descend or stop; going without an undervest could well cause rashes and chafing.

Lycra bib-type shorts are best, and should be worn next to the skin to avoid irritation. Bibs are better than conventional shorts as they do not have stomach-restricting elastic, and the 'bib' straps ensure they do not slip down and expose your lower back. Generally speaking, the more sections the shorts are cut in the better. Synthetic chamois is commonplace, and many shorts also have a protective terry pad. Shorts should be kept clean at all times, but avoid washing them with strong detergents. Above all, always invest in quality shorts: CoolMax is a good summer choice.

ABOVE: *In spring and autumn, when it is not quite warm enough for shorts, three-quarter-length bottoms, arm warmers and an extra undervest are an ideal compromise.*
LEFT: *This is the classic summer racing or training kit of shorts, short-sleeved jersey and short socks, with an undervest to 'wick away' the sweat.*

A lightweight poly-cotton race jersey is your best bet on top; the short neck zip acts as a thermostat to stop you from overheating. Try to avoid Lycra, as it tends to hold the sweat.

Ankle socks, made of either cotton or, better still, CoolMax are ideal for keeping your feet comfortable. Avoid riding without socks. Your shoes should fit properly and have plenty of ventilation (see pages 136–7).

One item without which you should never leave home is a race cape, or windproof jacket. Temperatures change quickly, showers occur, descents are cold, you stop. At any of these times, put on your jacket and avoid catching a chill. A breathable jacket is best: otherwise you will just sweat inside it, which will make it difficult to take off afterwards.

A great option in dry conditions is to carry a sleeveless gillet jacket, which will keep the chill away and is very compact to carry.

In hot conditions it is always advisable to wear either a cotton race cap or Buff style headband beneath your helmet, to soak up the sweat and keep the sun off your head.

Short track mitts are always a sensible move in any weather, especially if you are racing. When you fall your hands are almost always the first part of you to scrape the ground, and they take a long time to heal, so it's best to protect them.

Spring and autumn additions

Unless the temperatures are very high, you should avoid riding in summer 'race kit' alone. Leg and arm warmers are great for mild conditions, and are

ABOVE: *If you want to stay healthy, never leave home without a windproof jacket.*
LEFT: *Protective eyewear and a helmet are well worth investing in.*

easily stashed in your back pocket should the weather warm up. Three-quarter-length tights are also useful in this sort of weather, because they keep your knees warm whilst letting the calves get some air.

On top, you should be particularly careful, making sure that your chest and lungs are well protected from the chilly air: serious infection can be caused by overexposure. Add another undervest if in doubt, together with a long-sleeved jersey on top of your short-sleeved jersey. It is wise to adhere to this layering system, as opposed to just putting on a thick winter jacket.

In cool conditions, a lightweight headband is of great benefit, keeping you warm by preventing heat loss through the head without causing you to overheat.

Sunglasses

Good quality sunglasses are not just for posing. They are invaluable in any weather, but particularly when it is hot. Not only do they protect your eyes from grit, pollen, dust and flies, they also make it easier for you to see where you are going, and they provide protection from ultraviolet rays.

You do not have to pay vast amounts for good glasses, but cheaper ones are usually of inferior quality and have less UV protection, which can damage your eyes.

Winter clothing

Winter is a time of year when it is essential to choose the right garments for the weather conditions. Making the wrong decision can leave you in serious difficulties. Wind chill is usually the cyclist's biggest enemy; it is often considerably greater if you ride across high or exposed terrain.

As always, the layering system should be adhered to, starting with an effective base layer. A good sweat-wicking undervest is essential in order to keep your body warm and dry: this should be of a heavier weight than you would use in summer, and should probably be long-sleeved. A base layer of a similar material on your legs is also advisable if temperatures are below freezing or the wind chill is strong.

Just how many layers you wear will obviously depend on the temperature. Middle layers are usually best made up of short-sleeved or sleeveless and long-sleeved poly-cotton jerseys. Many riders prefer to keep their arms relatively unrestricted – hence the sleeveless jerseys.

Your choice of top layer will depend on the weather conditions. There are some great products on offer these days, and they are generally well worth investing in.

Your top layer should always be 'breathable', should cover your back,

A warm fleece hat is best in winter; clear or yellow glasses offer worthwhile eye protection. **LEFT:** *A breathable, lightweight Gore-Tex top will keep you comfortable when the weather gets really cold and wet.*

and should not be restrictive. In cold and windy conditions a micro-fleece style top with a Windstopper front is ideal. There are also some great mixed wool fibre jerseys available, ideal when it's dry.

If it's drizzling or windy then you will need to consider a well-vented Pertex or heavier option, but you must weigh the advantages against the sweat issue.

In winter, it is advisable never to leave home without a good wind proof

and showerproof jacket stashed in your pocket. Pertex-type material is ideal for insulation and wind-stopping purposes, but when the weather gets really bad a garment made from Gore-Tex or a similar material is called for. Gore-Tex is not ideal under normal conditions, as it simply does not breathe well enough and causes heavy sweating, but in extreme weather a Gore-Tex or similar material top, preferably with vented sides, is indispensable. Standard nylon rain capes are fine if you are not out for too long, and for warding off the occasional shower, but they have the suffocation effect of a plastic bag during prolonged use.

Extremities

Because of their lack of mobility and exposure to the wind, your hands, feet and head can be particularly vulnerable to the cold when riding in winter.

Your head and ears should always be well covered, at least when starting out. An oversized helmet with a headband/ thin fleece hat underneath is a good option. It is also advisable to wear protective glasses in winter: some manufacturers make clear lenses for rain and yellow lenses for dull days, which will fit into the same frames as the tinted lenses you use in summer.

Hands are best covered by gloves which are slightly on the large side, preferably with grippy pads and not-too-stiff fingers. Thinsulite-lined or Windstopper gloves are the best; in extreme cold, lightweight liners are also a good idea. Always try to keep your gloves dry: if wet they can become painfully cold.

For your feet, always add your

layers over your shoes: never cram your shoes with thick or double socks, as they restrict circulation. Try a pair of overshoes, although they are prone to making your feet sweat; Neoprene overshoes are the most effective at keeping feet warm and dry.

TOP: *Winter weather may be wet, dry, cold or windy: all call for different approaches to clothing, but protection from the elements is always essential.*
ABOVE LEFT: *Warm, grippy gloves that are not too tight are essential in winter.*
ABOVE: *Neoprene overshoes are probably the best all-rounders.*

Shoes and helmets

The feet and the head are two of the most important, and the most vulnerable, parts of a cyclist's body: it is vital that they are well protected and comfortable when you ride.

There are so many designs of helmets and shoes on sale that looking for the right thing can be a nightmare. Suitability, price, legality and fit should all be taken into consideration when you are making your choice. The ultimate decision is down to you, but here are a few pointers to help you.

Helmets

You should always wear a helmet when riding. In racing it is compulsory, and indeed in many countries it is illegal to ride without a helmet.

It is crucial to check out the safety standard stickers on the helmet, as different bodies have different minimum standards for competition helmets. Look out for the ANSI and SNELL stickers; CE is worthless. Aero helmets are also usually not up to recognised safety standards, and are worn mostly for aerodynamic as opposed to safety purposes.

Shoes

Although shoes may differ substantially in quality and looks, most modern racing shoes are fairly similar in design. Generally, new models can be used with most makes of clipless pedals and cleats, but it is worth double-checking before buying. (See pages 116–7 for more about the various types of pedals.)

TOP: *Aero helmets are permitted in time trials, but they are not usually designed with safety in mind.* ABOVE: *Good ventilation, comfort and protection are essential. This helmet with its Carrera team stickers, may look flashy, but any such decoration invalidates the guarantee, which may be a lifelong one.*

HELMET NOTES

1 Different makes of helmet can vary considerably in fit: try them first.
2 Helmets with extra protection for the back of the neck are safer in general.
3 The more ventilation there is, the better.
4 Look out for advantageous guarantees: some reputable manufacturers will give a life long low cost replacement guarantee for damaged helmets. But be warned: this is often invalidated if you put stickers on the helmet.
5 Aero helmets are great for aerodynamics, but not so good for protection.
6 Once a helmet is damaged, replace it.

SHOE POINTS

1 Make sure that the shoes are well vented, for letting in cool air and letting out water.
2 Shoes with carbon-fibre and Kevlar soles tend to be more expensive, but they are far more rigid and durable.
3 Velcro and ratchet fastening shoes are now almost standard: they are far more efficient and comfortable than lace-ups.

Make sure that you get the perfect fit before considering what the shoes look like.

Different shoes vary considerably in their fit – for instance, many Italian brands have a narrow fitting – so shop around if you find your feet are cramped at the sides. Aim to have just under an inch of room at the toe end when standing up. Check that the heels do not restrict your movement, but also that they are not too soft, causing your feet to slop around. Reinforced toes are usually more comfortable, too. If you have low arches, make sure that the soles are not too angled for comfort, and that the arches are not too high: there is a great deal of variation between makes and models.

Be very careful when trying out your new shoes for the first time, as sole thickness can vary by up to a centimetre, and some sole designs will push your feet out a touch from your cranks. This can have quite substantial effects on your normal riding position, and may even cause you knee and back pain; whose cause may be difficult to trace. However, it is easy to avoid these problems by measuring the distance from the inside of your clipped-in shoes to the top of the saddle and altering the saddle height and cleat position accordingly. When setting up new shoes and cleats it is a good idea to ease the tension on your pedal and not to over-tighten the cleats at first, as they may cause indentations in the sole, making it difficult to change afterwards. Also, be aware that they may move when you release from the pedal. With some brands it's possible to remove your feet from the shoe and tighten the cleat in situ. You should also always re-tighten your cleats after their first ride.

Tricks of the trade

Experienced cyclists have many inexpensive tricks to combat the weather and to make themselves that little bit more comfortable. You might never find out about them except by accident, yet most of them are born out of common sense.

Newspaper is a budget chest protector widely used by top riders for its convenience.

Riding into the wind is always particularly hazardous, because your chest is exposed to the cold. You may have seen Tour de France riders being given newspapers as they reach the top of Alpine passes; the papers are stuffed up the fronts of their jerseys to protect their chests from the chilling effect of the wind on the descent. In winter, many cyclists place a newspaper or even a plastic bag between their layers of clothing to combat the wind. Another way to achieve the benefits of an extra layer over the chest, without restricting the mobility of your arms, is to cut the sleeves out of a thick thermal top; alternatively, if you have money to spare, chamois chest protectors and thermal gilets are available.

Protecting the extremities

For early-season races, and when it is chilly but not excessively cold, many riders wear an old pair of racing socks over the top of their shoes, having cut a hole in the bottom for the cleat. This makes an ideal dry-weather substitute for overshoes.

In extreme cold, some riders put embrocation on their feet, and often on their knees and backs, although this can irritate the skin. If your feet

become severely chilled, get off and walk for a while to help your blood flow back into them.

In very wet and cold conditions, you could try wearing thin plastic bags over your socks to keep out the cold water. It is also a good idea to wear a thin pair of rubber washing-up gloves either over or under your normal pair: wet gloves are worse than none at all. Taking a spare pair of dry gloves is a good idea, and that goes for hats, too.

Beating the elements

If you do not have mudguards, a plastic bag down the back of your shorts will help to protect your back.

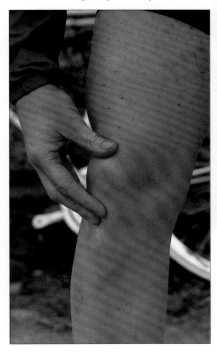

Putting silver foil beneath your helmet is a very efficient form of insulation, as is wrapping cling film over it, but this is advisable only in extreme cold.

In cold weather, and in fact at any time of year, if you intend to have a

ABOVE: *Covering your helmet in cling film will keep out cold air and rain.*
TOP: *Old socks with holes cut for your shoe cleats protect the feet in dry weather.*
LEFT: *Some riders put embrocation on their knees to keep them warm in winter.*

break during a ride it is a good idea to carry a lightweight spare undervest with you. Wrap it in a thin plastic bag and replace your sweaty one as soon as you are indoors: this greatly reduces the risk of catching a chill. Similarly, if you stop for a drink, strip off your

damp outer layers and hang them over the back of a chair or a radiator to dry them out before you start riding again.

In winter, you can risk dehydration caused by drinks freezing in your bottle. To avoid this, cut off the top of a large bottle, then take out the inside section of a child's thermos flask, pad it with bubble wrap and tape it inside the bottle. This will give you hot or warm drinks for at least a couple of hours, which could be invaluable in extreme cold.

CHAPTER 9

The road-bike workshop

For you to ride your fastest and win races, your bike must be in perfect condition and you must have complete

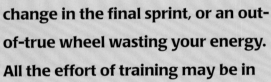

confidence in it. The last thing you need is a slipped gear

change in the final sprint, or an out-of-true wheel wasting your energy. All the effort of training may be in vain if your bike lets you down. The key is preventative maintenance. This chapter shows you how to make the routine checks and adjustments, and also how to modify your bike for particular events. Doing these jobs yourself soon pays for the tools; it can also be very satisfying, and you will have a bike that is always 100 per cent ready for winning.

Taking care of your bike

As you become familiar with your bike, you will develop an eye and ear for anything amiss. Always investigate it promptly: if you are in doubt about an adjustment, or cannot do it yourself, go to a good bike mechanic.

One of the vital factors in bike maintenance is your own attitude. It helps to be patient and analytical as you work; hurrying, getting angry (sometimes even the best mechanics can feel like kicking the bike) or not understanding what you are doing can cost you time and money. Stop if you become frustrated; coming back later with a fresh mind can help enormously.

The procedures described in this chapter are all fairly easy if they are approached with care. Ensure that tools fit properly. Be careful not to over-tighten small bolts, such as cable clamps, or to cross-thread items with fine threads, such as the tools used for crank removal, as the threads are easily stripped. On the other hand, some items, such as crank retaining bolts and the bottom-bracket cartridge, need to be tightened fully, or they may work loose over time.

If you are not sure how much to tighten something, ask a more experienced mechanic to show you — tools that measure the torque applied are not usually very practical on bicycles. But do not worry too much: once you have a little experience, you will soon acquire a 'feel' for what is right.

The working space

It is important to have a well-lit working space with room to move. If you are fortunate, you may be able to set aside a special area for this, such as part of a garage, utility room, garden shed or cellar. Many people make do with the kitchen: it is not too cold, the floor is usually easy to clean, you can wash your hands without spreading grease all round the house, and there is ample food and drink to keep you going!

A small work bench and a wall-mounted tool board (painted white, with nails to hook the tools onto and outlines to show what goes where) are useful if you have space. If you cannot run to a permanent workshop area, a tool tray or rack, for keeping the most frequently used items at hand, is a good idea.

A work stand avoids the need for a great deal of improvisation. Because the bike is held at a convenient height, it is easy to see exactly what is going

A good work stand, as shown here, makes maintenance jobs much easier.

A professional mechanic prepares his team's bikes before the start of a race.

on. If you can afford it, buy a solid stand with plenty of scope for adjustment. Cheaper alternatives simply lift the back wheel off the ground, or clamp onto a work bench. Beware of clamping a very thin tube too tightly, or around a braze-on, as this may dent it. The seat post is usually a secure and safe clamp point.

Another useful workshop item is a track pump. This is a great labour-saving device for inflating racing tyres quickly to very high pressures, and usually has a built-in pressure gauge, which is invaluable. Ordinary frame pumps are prone to bend the valve, and often struggle to reach the recommended pressures.

Non-routine maintenance

If you use your bike regularly, any bearings of the traditional 'cup and cone' design (in most cases the hubs and headset, and possibly the pedals) should be stripped down and overhauled at least once a year. Worn parts are replaced, bearings need to be packed with clean grease, and the component must be adjusted precisely to minimise friction and wear and to avoid rapid component failure. *The Bike Book* (Haynes Publishing, 1995)

explains how to do this.

If any of your components contain sealed cartridge bearings, the cartridges or (in the case of lower-quality components) the complete unit may need to be replaced. Typically, cartridge bearings last about three years and are replaced as soon as play, roughness or noise, such as squeaking, is detected. (Some hubs have a minute amount of play built in.) Replacing cartridge bearings is probably best left to your dealer.

Workshop basics: what you need

You do not need many tools for basic maintenance. Those shown here will allow you to carry out all the adjustments and checks described in this chapter, and will virtually cover you for a complete overhaul.

*I*t pays to buy the best you can afford, but, in general, 'consumer'-quality workshop tools are perfectly adequate. Buy a set of Allen keys from a good tool shop: you will need 4mm, 5mm and 6mm sizes, along with others to fit your particular bike. Multi-angle Allen keys are best, as they reach awkward corners. A Y-shaped Allen key with three different-sized ends is a useful addition.

You will also need a few basic household tools. Adjustable spanners are useful for applying leverage, but not normally recommended for small nuts. Small spanners are needed for some brakes and fitments: ring (crown) spanners are best, as they do not slip. A soft mallet, or a hammer used with a wooden block for protection, is also necessary.

Cassette and chain tools

Cassettes are normally removed with a cassette tool and chain wrench; the Pamir Hyper-Cracker is a cheap, light but fiddly alternative. A ruler can be used to measure chain wear, but Roloff or Park chain calibres are quicker and more accurate.

Chainset, bottom-bracket and headset tools

The advent of the threadless headset has made adjustment a lot easier these days. All you need are the relevant Allen keys to set up, adjust and replace bearings. Some models will still require a press to replace fork and frame cups; this can be done with a soft rubber mallet, but is best done by an experienced mechanic.

Older style threaded headsets will require a pair of specialist oversized flat spanners to make adjustments.

In recent years bottom bracket and crank designs have changed a lot. Many cranks are not fixed on to splined axles, making maintenance easy with simple Allen keys. Many older models still work on a tapered system for removal and replacement. For these you will need a dedicated crank puller and bolt removal tool/oversized Allen key.

Most

modern bottom bracket units are removed with a special splined tool and a large adjustable spanner, while older systems will still require oversized spanners to remove the cups, and a double pin spanner to set the adjustable cup.

Brake, gear and cable tools

Special bicycle cable cutters are designed to cut both the inner cable and the cable housing, and to crimp on cable end caps. Good-quality side cutters, designed for cutting wire, will do the same job. A cable puller tensions and holds the cable in place while the cable clamp is tightened; alternatively you can use a pair of pliers.

Spares

You should keep a small stock of the most essential spares: two inner tubes, a tyre, rear brake and gear cables and brake blocks should be enough. A few cable end caps are always useful to prevent cable ends fraying. Buy a

puncture-repair kit with feather-edged patches, as these work best on narrow tubes.

Consumables

Sticky, tenacious bike oils, such as Finish Line, are best for wet-weather chain lubrication, but collect dirt; do not use 3:1 oils (often containing vegetable oil combined with petroleum distillate), as these are too thin and tend to gum up. PTFE (Teflon) sprays are good 'clean' general-purpose lubricants, especially for gear and brake-pivot assemblies. They are also good for chains in dry conditions. Petroleum distillate sprays, such as WD40, repel water and generally free up moving parts. For completely seized parts, use PlusGas, available from motor shops.

Special bike greases are best for bearings and are also good for cables and general assembly. Anti-

seize grease prevents assembled titanium parts or aluminium and steel from 'cold welding' together. A drop of thread-lock compound applied to bolt threads prevents unwanted loosening.

Biodegradable degreasers should be used to remove old grease and oil — they are better for you and for the environment. Industrial hand cleaners, such as Swarfega or, better still, Loctite Fast Orange, get the grimiest hands clean. Applying barrier cream before working offers protection, helps prevent dermatitis and makes your hands easier to clean.

• •

WHEEL TOOLS AND ALLEN KEYS: 1 spoke key; **2** Allen keys; **3** cone spanners for hub bearing adjustment; **4** tyre levers
CHAIN AND CASSETTE TOOLS: 5 chain tool; **6** chain wrench; **7** cassette tool/freewheel remover; **8** cassette cracker; **9** chain calibre.
CHAINSET, BOTTOM BRACKET AND HEADSET TOOLS: 10 adjustable peg spanner; **11** crank-bolt tool; **12** bottom-bracket cartridge tool; **13** crank extractor; **14** headset spanner; **15** combined pedal and headset spanner; **16** chainring back-nut spanner.
BRAKE, GEAR AND CABLE TOOLS: 17 cable puller ('fourth hand'); **18** cable cutters; **19** brake centring tool

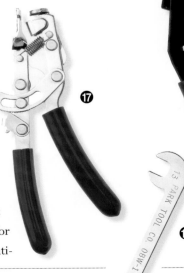

Cleaning and inspection

Grit, and in particular winter road salt, will wear and corrode your bike, so you should give it a good clean and inspection about once a week, as well as in preparation for races. Look for potential faults as you go along.

If possible, put the bike in a work stand to clean it, and remove the wheels. Hook the chain onto the chain hanger (the small peg at the bottom of the seat stay), if your frame has one. If the bike is particularly dirty, spray the worst and most hard-to-reach areas with a biodegradable degreaser, avoiding the bearings, and leave for 20 minutes before proceeding.

Prepare a bucket of hot water with a generous squirt of dish detergent. Work methodically along the bike from the bars to the rear derailleur, using a large sponge, toothbrush and bottle-brush, as appropriate, to reach everywhere and loosen the dirt. A stiff floor brush is good for the tyres. Rinse with cold water from top to bottom, using a sponge kept specially for this purpose. Wipe or shake off excess

water and let the bike dry. Polish the frame with either car wax or a special bike polish and protector. This helps it to shed water and dirt, making it easier to keep clean, and guards against rust.

Apply small quantities of a PTFE (Teflon) based spray (using the little straw supplied) to the brake and derailleur pivot points and inside the brake levers.

Chain care

A dirty chain is inefficient, wears the transmission and shifts badly. However, do not clean the chain more often than necessary, as the manufacturer's lubrication deep inside its bushings will be dispersed and subsequent lubrication may be less effective.

After a long, wet ride, lightly spray the chain with WD40 to prevent

rust and stiff links. The chain is best cleaned with a special device designed for this purpose, which holds a small amount of degreaser; this is attached and the pedals are rotated, cleaning the chain in minutes (see photograph below left). Afterwards, wipe the chain and let it dry. A wire brush will remove any stubborn grime.

Clean any accumulated gunge off the cassette cogs, derailleur pulley wheels and chainset. Now is a good time to check the wear. Excessive chain wear (play in the links) is indicated if, with the chain under load, 24 links, from centre rivet to centre rivet, measure over 308mm. If the cassette is worn, it will probably need replacing at the same time, to avoid the new chain jumping.

Never let the chain get completely dry, but neither should it drip with oil, as this only gathers more dirt. Put the chain on a middle cog and rotate the pedals slowly while dripping the oil onto the centre of the chain. Whizz the pedals round to help disperse it.

Chain removal and fitting

The same procedure applies whether you are fitting a new chain or replacing damaged chain links. If possible, keep

A special chain-cleaning device makes the process simpler and less messy.

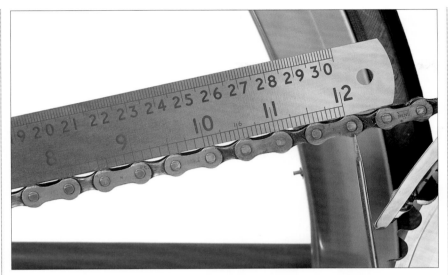

LEFT: *Use a ruler to assess chain wear.*
BELOW: CHAIN REMOVAL The pin is screwed in until it almost pushes the rivet out of the link. Ensure the rivet is not obstructed by the back of the tool or you will deform the link, or break the tool.
BOTTOM: CHAIN FITTING Wiggle and twist the chain slightly to snap it back together.

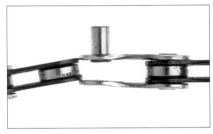

a separate chain for each different cassette you use (see page 150). A new chain may need to be shortened: consult your dealer about this.

To remove a chain first lay it into the slot on the chain tool; most chains now have special hyper/power links to join and break them, these are usually a different colour to the rest of the chain. It is easier to break and join the chain at these points.

Align the chain pin with the push-pin in the tool and tighten, pushing the rivet through. In most instances you should avoid pushing the rivet right through if you intend to rejoin the chain. If the chain is joined by a specific link then you can push the

rivet out and rejoin with a new pin. If the rivet is still in place wiggle the chain sideways to break it.

To fit a chain you should first break it to the correct length, usually the same as the old one. Put the chain in place, but not on the front chain ring, and if the rivet is in place click it together by hand, and then push it through with the tool until the rivet has equal overlap on either side. With a specific pin, as used by Shimano, push the rivet through in the same way and then break off the excess section with pliers.

Stiff links created where a chain has been rejoined, or caused by insufficient cleaning and lubrication, may be freed by putting the link on the near slot of the chain tool and pushing the pin through a fraction; this will spread the outer plates.

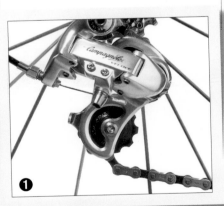

❶

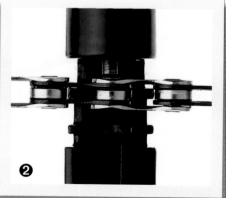

❷

STIFF LINKS ❶ Back-pedal the chain to find stiff links; these will lift up from the derailleur pulley wheels. ❷ With the chain on this slot, the pin pushes the plates apart.
LEFT: SHIMANO CHAINS The pin has been pushed through point first, and the protruding part can be snapped off using pliers. You can see the groove pin on the spare pin alongside.

Quick-releases and hubs

A quick-release must be set up properly to save time and – more importantly – for your safety.

When removing wheels, first open up the brake's quick-release to avoid the tyre snagging against the brake blocks.

For rear wheels, shift the chain onto the smallest front and rear cogs. Pull the quick-release lever fully open, with its inner curve facing outwards. Lift the bike, pull the chain and rear derailleur clear and let the wheel drop out. A small thump on the tyre may be necessary.

Front wheels are removed in a similar manner, but you may need to contend with 'safety' forks. These have retaining lips which require you to open the quick-release fully, then loosen off the knurled nut on the opposite side a few turns to release the wheel.

Before fitting a wheel, check that the quick-release lever is fully open, with its inner curve facing outwards. By convention, both front and rear levers are always on the left of the bike.

To fit the rear wheel, put the top part of the chain over the smallest cog and let the bottom part hang below. Keeping the derailleur back, pull the wheel fully into the drop-outs; then close the quick-release so that it points back and up or between the stays. This movement should feel firm but not require excessive force. Leave

release in line with the fork blade, with a small gap between them. If you have 'safety' lips on your forks, you will need to readjust the quick-release by tightening the knurled nut a few turns.

If your drop-outs and frame are perfectly aligned, your wheel should centralise in the frame. If it does not,

OPENING THE BRAKE ❶ On Shimano brakes, lift the small lever by the cable clamp bolt. ❷ On Campagnolo brakes, depress the small button at the top of the brake lever.

enough finger space for when you next open it.

Fitting front wheels is done in much the same way: close the quick-

hold it in alignment as you close the quick-release. Horizontal drop-outs should have adjusters that can be pre-set to give the correct alignment.

Hub checks

With the wheel in the frame or forks, grasp the rim and try to wobble it

REMOVING A REAR WHEEL The fingers of the right hand pull back the derailleur, while the thumbs ease the wheel out of the drop-outs.

tighten the locknut down on it. This usually results in the bearings coming slightly loose again, so some trial and error may be necessary to achieve the perfect adjustment. If no matter what you do the bearings remain rough, or tight in one spot and loose in another, the hub should be overhauled (see page 143).

After a year or so of regular use, the bearings may become dry inside and need regreasing. This is indicated by a very loose feeling as you turn the correctly adjusted axle, or if you can hear ticking sounds. Campagnolo Record and post-1995 Chorus hubs can be regreased with a grease gun without needing to be disassembled; rotate the central clip, then pump grease through until clean grease emerges.

from side to side. Any play at the rim generally indicates loose bearings in the hub. Take out the wheel and remove its quick-release unit: to do this, unscrew the knurled nut completely and pull the quick-release free. Do not lose the conical springs, whose narrow ends face inwards; these align the unit within the hub. Next, turn and wobble the axle by hand; grating, excessive friction or play show that adjustment is needed. A trace of play is normal, and is taken up by the compression of the secured quick-release.

Shimano and Campagnolo hubs contain conventional ball bearings. The adjustable cones, which regulate the play of the bearings, are largely hidden from view inside the hub. They are held in place by an outer locknut.

Adjustment is made on the left-hand cone only. Holding the cone with a correctly fitting cone spanner,

loosen the outer locknut with another spanner; a second cone spanner may be necessary, as the flat edges are often recessed. Set the cone just a little tighter than finger tight and

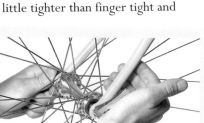

WHEEL FITTING: ❶ Keep the wheel firmly in place as you close the quick-release. ❷ To reduce the effort needed to close the quick-release, open it up and back off the knurled nut. Tighten the nut to make the action firmer. LEFT: ADJUSTING THE BEARINGS The cone spanner holds the cone while the adjustable spanner is used to loosen the locknut.

Cassettes, spokes and rims

For different events, you are likely to want to fit cassettes with different combinations of cogs. Wheels need to be checked regularly for broken spokes and to make sure they are running true.

It is best to have a separate chain for each cassette, as the cassette and chain wear in and wear out together. Look out for broken or bent teeth on the cogs, and periodically check that the lockring is tight.

To remove a cassette, first fit the cassette removal tool into the splines of the lockring. Use the quick-release,

CASSETTE REMOVAL ❶ Position the lockring tool, making sure it engages with at least 2mm of spline. ❷ With the chain wrench, lockring tool and spanner in place, push hard against the floor.

• •

with the springs removed, to keep the tool fully seated. With the wheel against your legs, position a chain wrench on the left-hand side of the second-largest cog so that you are pushing down and clockwise. Use a large adjustable spanner on the lockring tool to act in the opposite direction. Push until the lockring gives.

Remove the quick-release and spin the lockring free. Lift off the smallest cog, the shim (thin washer) if applicable, the second cog and the

CASSETTE REPLACEMENT ❶ Align the triangular mark on top of Sachs and Shimano cassette bodies with the wide spline and slide it on. ❷ Fit Campagnolo cogs so that the triangular marks on each of the cogs are in line and the 'O' marks run clockwise (unless you have replaced some of the cogs with ones of different sizes to those originally supplied as a set).

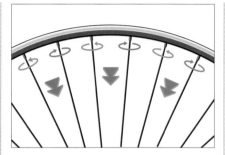

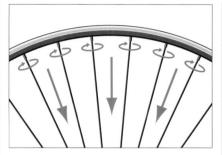

CORRECTING SIDEWAYS WOBBLE Loosen the spokes that connect to the hub flange on the side the wheel wobbles towards, and tighten those on the other side by an equal amount.
FAR LEFT: CORRECTING POOR CONCENTRICITY: Tighten the spokes to bring the rim in, loosen them to let it out.

cassette body. Campagnolo cogs and their spacers are not attached, and are all removed individually.

When replacing a cassette, first ensure that the cassette body, or the cogs and their spacers, are thoroughly clean. Slide it/them on, followed by the smallest cogs and shim (if you removed one). Use the lockring tool to screw on the lockring, refit the quick-release and tighten the lockring firmly with a large adjustable spanner; you will normally hear a number of distinctive clicks.

Spoke and rim checks

Spin the wheels, looking for side-to-side and concentric (up-down) movement of the rim in excess of 1mm. If the rim is out of true, it is usually a sign of uneven spoke tension.

Wheel truing requires skill, so practise on old wheels! Truing of deep section, radial-spoked and high-tension factory wheels is very tricky, and best left to professional mechanics.

Remove the tyre and tube. Examine the wheel as a whole, looking for the spots where it is most out. Where the rim bulges outwards (showing poor concentricity), it needs to be pulled in. This is done by using a spoke key to tighten the spokes under the high spot by about half a turn at most — less towards the edges of the bulge. Do the

reverse where the rim dips inwards.

Where the rim moves sideways, loosen the spokes that radiate from the hub flange on that side by about a quarter of a turn, and tighten the ones on the opposite side by the same amount. Again, spread the adjustments over several spokes, with less adjustment to those further from the worst point. Repeat as required. Very small adjustments may be necessary for perfection.

When you have finished, pluck the spokes in turn. They should all ring with an even, bright sound, not a dull

twang, though the left side of the rear wheel may sound a lot duller. If the wheel and/or the spoke tension are too far out, an expert wheel true or rebuild might be called for.

Rim wear

Modern rims have very thin walls, and brake blocks continually wear them thinner. In time, this can become dangerous, as the tyre pressure can make the rim split suddenly. If the braking surface has a channel or other signs of wear more than 0.5mm deep, you are advised to replace the rim.

A wheel-truing jig holds the wheel firmly in place and has adjustable reference points. Alternatively, put the wheel in the bike in the work stand. Cocktail sticks can be tacked on the seat stays to form adjustable reference points.

Tyres and tubulars

Tube repair must be 100 per cent efficient for racing. A loose patch, hot weather or an attempt to repair anything other than a very small hole may result in the patch blowing off or the tube slowly deflating. If in any doubt, fit a new tube.

To remove a tyre, remove the dust cap and retaining ring and completely deflate the tube. Push the valve up into the tyre to free it. Insert a tyre lever opposite the valve. Fit another beside it and slide it around the rim on that side, lifting off the complete bead, then pull the tube free. Look for cuts, damage and debris embedded in the tyre treads and side walls. Also check for protruding spokes or a rough rim joint and file smooth if necessary.

Fitting a tyre

First, ensure that the rim tape is centred and in good condition. Fit the tyre around one bead, then inflate the tube until it is just round and fit the valve through the rim, lifting the tyre back over it. Push the tube neatly into place, keeping the valve straight. Starting at the valve, use your thumbs to fit the second tyre bead. If it is tight, deflate the tube a little. Push the valve up into the tyre to seat it correctly.

Using your thumbs only, slide the last bit of tyre on. Check that the tube is not caught under the tyre bead, and free it if necessary. Inflate to about 1.5 bar (20psi) and spin the wheel. If the bead line does not follow the rim edge, push and pull the tyre into

place. Inflate the tyre to full pressure (shown on the tyre wall), then replace the retaining ring and dust cap.

Repairing a tube

Find the hole by inflating the tube to twice its normal size. Listen or feel for escaping air; if this does not work, hold the tube under water and look for bubbles. Mark the hole with converging pen lines. Fully deflate the tube and make sure it's completely dry, then roughen an area around the hole twice the size of your patch. Apply a thin film of rubber solution, wait until it is touch dry and apply another. When dry, peel off the backing from the patch and centre the patch on the hole. Rub it down firmly,

REMOVING A TYRE ❶ The tyre levers are used to hook the tyre off the rim. Narrow tyres can be tricky to remove, owing to their tight fit. ❷ If you had a puncture, carefully feel inside the tyre until you find the cause (a thorn or piece of glass, for instance) or are sure there is nothing there.

TYRE FITTING ❶ Fit one complete tyre bead, work the tube underneath it, then lift the second bead onto the rim. ❷ Always use your thumbs, not tyre levers, to fit a tyre.

TUBE REPAIR ❶ The rubber solution should be touch dry before the patch is applied. ❷ Peel off the cellophane from the centre outwards.

. . . .

With the tubular slightly inflated, fit the valve. Then push the tyre onto the rim, working down both sides at once. Use your thumbs to get the last bit on. Push and pull the tubular to align it, then inflate it firm and check the alignment again, correcting it if necessary. Leave the wheel for a few hours before riding.

A previously used tubular with a residual coating of cement can be fitted without extra cement to get you home after a puncture: ride very gently to avoid it rolling off.

Repairing tubulars is a tricky job: it is best to send the tyre to a specialist repair service.

then fold and crack the cellophane and peel it off from the centre outwards. Dust the repair with chalk powder.

Tubulars

A new tubular should be fitted to an unprepared rim and inflated to stretch it before use. Store tubulars on rims or wheels, off the ground.

Normally, rim cement is used to stick a tubular to the rim. You may also come across special double-sided tape, which is cleaner but less suitable for hard use.

Clean off old cement or tape with paint thinners and buff the surface of the rim with a wire brush. Apply a thin layer of cement to the concave rim well, avoiding the braking surface. Leave it to dry, then apply a second layer. Inflate the tubular until it is just firm and apply cement to its base tape. Leave everything until the cement is a little less than tacky.

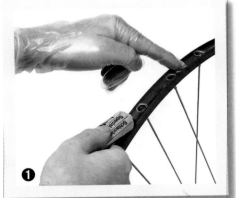

FITTING A TUBULAR ❶ It is sensible to wear washing-up or surgical gloves while applying rim cement, as it does not come off your hands easily. Avoid getting cement on the braking surface. ❷ Push the tubular down, keeping it under constant tension.

The gears

Sluggish shifting or poor indexing is usually a cable problem. If your chain comes off, on the other hand, the derailleur's limit screws need to be adjusted. You should always make the checks in the order described below. (See pages 110–111 for details of the gearing components.)

First, remove the wheel and operate the gear shifters; if the derailleurs do not move with precise, steady and free movement in both directions, and if you are sure it is not the derailleur itself that is stiff, you need to fit a new inner cable. Replace the casing if it is more than a year old.

Before removing the derailleur cable, note its routing and its mounting under the derailleur's cable clamp. Shift the gears to the smallest front and rear cogs, pushing the levers as far over as they will go so that they are fully retracted. Loosen the cable clamp to free the cable and remove it.

Set the cable adjusters on both the derailleur and down tube at two turns unscrewed. Cut the new cable cleanly with cable cutters, and fit an end cap on each end. Grease the cable and nipple, then feed the cable into the gear shifter and through the system; tighten the cable clamp. Finally, cut off any excess cable and fit an end cap (see page 159).

Rear derailleur adjustment

Both front and rear derailleurs have limit screws. These pre-set their maximum sideways movement for the highest and lowest gears, and are often marked 'H' and 'L'. The low-limit screw is the lower of the pair on Shimano rear derailleurs (see photograph above right). On Campagnolo derailleurs it is the upper one.

The derailleur's top pulley should be set as close as it can go to the largest rear cog without catching. Unscrewing the B-tension screw

LEFT: *Loosening the cable clamp* RIGHT: *Cut new cable casing to size to give smooth bends.*

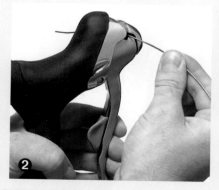

REPLACING THE CABLE ❶ With Campagnolo Ergopower shifters, you feed the cable in from below; ❷ with Shimano STI shifters, you pull the brake lever back slightly and feed the cable through from the side. ❸ Use a cable puller to take up the slack, release it slightly so that the cable is just taut and tighten the clamp.

reduces the gap. Screw in the low-limit screw until gear shifting into the largest rear cog becomes hesitant, then unscrew it one eighth of a turn.

Next, check that the pulley clears the smallest cog, again adjusting the B-tension screw if necessary. Screw the derailleur's cable adjuster fully in to slacken off the cable. The high-limit screw ('H') should now be screwed in until gear changing into the smallest cog becomes hesitant, then unscrewed one eighth of a turn. Ignore problems with the indexing at this stage.

Cable adjustment

You will need to set the indexing after any work on the rear derailleur and if the chain chatters or mis-shifts.

Shift into the larger chainring. Shift into the smallest rear cog, if it will not shift, or is hesitant, unscrew the cable adjuster until it does. Now shift to the second rear cog, if it will not shift or is hesitant unscrew the cable adjuster until it does. Next, unscrew the adjuster further, until the chain chatters against the third cog; then screw the adjuster back in until the noise just disappears. All the gears should now index perfectly; if you cannot get the largest rear cog cleanly, unscrew the rear

derailleur's low-limit screw an eighth of a turn at a time until you can.

Front derailleur adjustment

First, check that the outer cage plate's closest point clears the larger chainring by 1–2mm and is parallel to it. To reposition it, detach the cable (as described above), loosen the mounting clamp on the seat tube to make the adjustment, and then re-attach the cable.

Shift into the largest rear cog. Screw in the front derailleur's low-limit screw ('L') until the chain will just shift down to the smaller chainring without hesitation and without rubbing the cage. If it hesitates, unscrew the screw slightly.

❶ *Screwing in the low-limit screw.*

❷ *Screwing in the high-limit screw.*

❸ *Unscrewing the cable adjuster moves the derailleur's index points inwards.*

· ·

Reset the cable tension so that with the lever fully retracted it is just pulling taut. Now shift to the smallest rear cog. Screw in the high-limit screw ('H') until the shift up to the larger chainring becomes hesitant. Then unscrew it half a turn at a time until the shift just becomes clean.

Finally, if you have a triple chainset and Shimano STI levers, shift the chain to the middle chainring and largest rear cog. Use the down-tube adjuster to position the front derailleur's inner plate 0.5mm from the chain.

LEFT: *Here, the low-limit screw is the lower of the two. Note that the position of the limit screws is reversed on some models.* RIGHT: *The high-limit screw.*

The chainset, bottom bracket and pedals

Cranks sometimes need to be removed to allow you to make checks or adjustments to the bottom-bracket bearings and to replace chainrings. Do this only when necessary, as crank threads are easily damaged. Never ride on a loose crank: the high torque will almost immediately and irrevocably destroy its fit.

Many modern cranks use ISIS/splined systems, which make removal and maintenance quite easy. If you need to remove splined cranks then you need to either remove the bolt on the end of the axle or loosen the bolt on the crank, and then simply pull the crank off. To refit, clean the axle and crank thoroughly with degreaser first, and always make sure cranks are tight and are checked every few weeks.

Some cranks use the taper wedge system; to remove these you must remove the end bolt and then carefully screw the puller tool into the crank as far as it will go (being sure the puller is screwed open).

Screw the puller in against the axle to remove. Before refitting be sure to clean the crank and axle. Then tighten hard, and check that it's still tight after the first few rides.

Bottom-bracket maintenance

Modern bottom bracket units are often sealed, and are thus very low maintenance. Even so, it is worth periodically checking that the cups are tight by using the required tool.

Traditional style brackets are often of a cup and bearing design, which do require periodical maintenance, especially after wet weather. You should regularly check these brackets by unshipping the chain and seeing if

there is any movement in the cranks, and making sure that they feel smooth when spun.

If there is any disturbance then remove the cranks and, using the dedicated bracket tool, remove the left-hand lock ring and cup, and then re-grease or replace the bearings before reassembling the unit and clamping the lock ring tight. These units inevitably loosen up a little after use, so keep an eye on them.

Chainring checks

Bent, worn or damaged chainrings can cause the chain to jump, snag and rub irritatingly on your front derailleur. Chainrings can appear bent if the crank

USING A CRANK EXTRACTOR ❶ Ensure that the inner part of the crank extractor is fully retracted, then start the outer part into the greased crank threads – do not cross-thread it! – and tighten until firm. ❷ Screw in the inner part of the tool. Keep tightening past the point where resistance is met until the crank is eased off the axle, then remove the tool from the crank.

TIGHTENING THE RETAINING CUPS Left-hand cups tighten clockwise. Right-hand (chainset-side) cups normally tighten anticlockwise. Note that on bikes built for the Italian market they tighten clockwise.

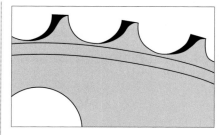

When worn, chainring teeth become thinner and can take on a pointed or, eventually, hooked shape.

CHAINRING REPAIRS A slightly bent chainwheel can be tweaked straight with an adjustable spanner

• •

is poorly fitted, so try refitting it first. Crooked teeth, in particular, can cause the chain to jump or catch; use an adjustable spanner to bend them back. You may have to remove the inner ring and hold it in a vice to do this.

Removing and fitting chainrings

Note the position of any spacing pieces between the rings before removing the chainring fixing bolts. Clean and then grease all the mounting points. Position

the chainrings to be fitted with their correct side facing outwards. Apply low-strength thread-lock compound to each bolt and assemble loosely. Finally, tighten each bolt in turn a little at a time, until they are all tight.

Pedals

Modern clipless pedals tend to have a long life, without the need for bearing adjustment or overhaul. However, you should refit pedals occasionally, as they can seize into the cranks. All right pedals have a right-hand thread, and the axle end is usually stamped 'R' or 'D'. All left pedals have a left-hand thread, and they are usually stamped 'L' or 'G'; they often have a knurled axle end to help start the thread.

Undo the right pedal anticlockwise and the left pedal clockwise. A lot of effort may be needed before anything budges: when it does, it will be sudden, so beware the sharp chainring teeth. Apply anti-seize grease to the axles and refit the correct pedal to each crank.

If getting your shoe into or out of the pedal becomes difficult, clean the pedal's release mechanism with a stiff wire brush and spray a little quick drying lubricant into the mechanism.

If you still have problems, you will need to replace the cleats or the pedal's 'body plate'.

TOP: REMOVING CHAINRING BOLTS Use a back-nut spanner to stop the nuts revolving.
ABOVE: REMOVING PEDALS Position yourself to get maximum leverage without the crank moving.

The end of the pedal axle is normally stamped for left /right identification.

• •

CREAKING

Irritating creaking or ticking sounds can often emanate from a slightly loose chainring bolt, crank, pedal or bottom-bracket cup. A dry interface between the components can be part of the cause. Reassemble them with a smear of grease on all the touching surfaces. In the case of cranks, this is a last resort – try tightening them really firmly first.

• •

The brakes

Brakes need frequent maintenance to ensure absolute reliability: braking should be smooth and progressive, yet powerful when needed. To achieve this, the brake pivot points should be free but without play, the wheels should be centralised and the rims true and clean.

There is a tendency for brake blocks to collect grit, which wears the rims and makes braking less effective, so pick any such foreign bodies out, particularly when the braking feels rough. Replace the blocks when the grooves have worn away or the wear line is reached.

When fitting new brake blocks,

you to point the brake block inwards so that its front end meets the rim 1mm before its rear. This 'toe-in' prevents squealing and vibration and improves braking power. Make sure the block follows the rim curve, with 1mm of clear braking surface above it. Tighten the mounting bolt firmly.

Check that your brake levers are

Cable replacement

The cable casing should be undamaged and without kinks, and the cable itself should show no signs of fraying. Before replacing the cable, screw the cable adjuster fully in. (Campagnolo ones work in the opposite direction to normal.) Cut new cable casing to size, allowing for smooth bends but not

ALTERNATIVE LAST RESORT TOE-IN METHOD Bend the brake arm in towards (or away from) the rim a little, using an adjustable spanner – but be very gentle!
LEFT: *Tightening the brake block.*
BELOW: *The brake-lever clamp bolt is either under the hood, as here, or inside the lever.*

check their orientation. If there are arrows on them, they should be positioned to point in the direction of the wheel's rotation. Some blocks have an angled profile, the wider edge being the lower one. Some brake shoes have an open end: this must face backwards.

Fit the conical washer (if there is one) on the inside and the plain washer on the outside. Conical washers allow

tightly attached to the bars by twisting the lever body sideways; make sure they are level by running a straight edge between the hood tops and checking that this is parallel with the bars. If the levers are not in a comfortable position for you, loosen the clamp bolt, reposition them and then re-tighten, but note that it is easy to overtighten and break the clamp, so take care.

FITTING A CABLE **❶** A cable puller is the best way to hold the brake closed and to take up slack in the system while tightening the cable clamp. **❷** Fine tune the brake-block position using the cable adjuster. **❸** After cutting off excess cable with cable cutters, use them to crimp on a cable end cap.

leaving it too long. Fit metal or plastic end caps to the cable casing where it enters the lever and if possible where it goes into any closed end such as cable guides or adjusters. Grease the inner cable and nipple and thread the cable through the system.

With the brake's quick-release closed (see page 148), thread the inner cable through the cable-clamp eye or slot. Use a cable puller to take up all excess cable and ensure the cable casing is seated firmly in its guides. Release the cable to let the blocks out to about 1mm from the rim. Now fully tighten the clamp.

Pull hard on the brake lever ten times to take up any remaining slack. If the blocks are now further out, un-screw the cable adjuster to bring them in to about 2mm from the rim. The brake should be easy to apply, powerful

if necessary, and with a little extra pull available should something slip.

Centralising

To centralise single-pivot and Campagnolo dual-pivot brakes, use a cone spanner or dedicated tool on the special flat edges, designed for this purpose, towards the rear of the brake. A brake can also be centralised by

loosening the nut attaching it to the frame, repositioning the brake and tightening the nut up again. Shimano dual-pivot brakes have a centralising mark that should point directly upwards; reposition them using the attachment bolt. Fine adjustment can be made by tightening the small screw on the side to bring the brake arms towards you, or loosening it to push them away.

CENTRALISING A BRAKE This is done either **❶** with a dedicated spanner, or **❷** by using the side adjustment screw on a Shimano dual-pivot brake.

The saddle, handlebars and headset

It is vital that your seat post and saddle are properly fitted. A sudden movement could make you lose control; a gradual creeping of the position could lose you a race. A badly adjusted or worn headset impairs the handling.

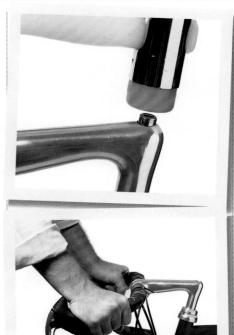

Seat posts are notorious for seizing into the frame, so liberally grease the hidden part with anti-seize grease. Set the saddle height you want, but do not exceed the maximum height mark: keep at least 5cm of post in the frame. Making sure the saddle is in line with the top tube, tighten the greased clamp bolt. The inside diameter of seat tubes varies: the post must be a perfect fit, both for security and to avoid damaging the frame.

Different rules apply with carbon frames and/or posts. These should be completely free of grease and impurities, and never over-tightened. Sometimes carbon posts are prone to slipping. Make sure they are clean and use wire wool to take the shine off the section inside the frame; this should help to reduce slips. With the saddle clamp loose enough to allow free movement, set the saddle as far forward or back as you require. With the bike on a level floor, use a spirit level to make sure the top of the saddle is horizontal. Some models of clamp have serrations, which may not allow fine adjustment of the angle. After greasing, tighten single-bolt

TOP: FREEING THE STEM BOLT Use a soft mallet, or otherwise protect the bolt.
BOTTOM: HANDLEBAR ADJUSTMENT Use force to check that the bars cannot twist downwards if you hit a bump.

....

clamps fully, or with twin-bolt designs give each bolt in turn a few twists until firm. The saddle will tilt towards the bolt you are tightening, so keep noting its position.

Handlebar stem adjustment

With threadless type stems handlebar height is adjusted by moving spacers from under or above the stem. If sufficient adjustment is not possible this way it is necessary to buy a new stem with a different rise. To move the spacers remove the allen bolt in the middle of the stem and the adjusting cap completely. Loosen the allen bolts

FITTING A SEAT POST The seat post must not twist, but do not over-tighten the bolt, as it may stretch the clamp.

Adjusting the saddle cradle with the help of a spirit level.

TRADITIONAL STYLE HEADSET ADJUSTMENT The adjustable race is held in place by the lower spanner, while the upper spanner loosens the locknut.

THREADLESS HEADSET ADJUSTMENT The allen bolt in the retaining cap adjusts the play in the headset. The stem securing bolts lock that adjustment

at the rear of the stem. Remove any spacers above the stem. Pull firmly upwards on the bars and stem which should slide off fairly easily. Replace the spacers so as to raise or lower the bars as you want. Remove the spacers below the stem if you want the bars lower. Add spacers below the stem if you want to raise the bars. Fit any spare spacers on top of the stem, do not leave any out. Refit the adjusting cap. The headset will now need adjusting – see the next section.

To adjust the handlebar angle with either type of stem, loosen the clamp

bolt and rotate the bars to the desired angle. Then grease and carefully re-tighten the bolt.

With traditional headset type stems undo the expander bolt about 5mm. You may have to give it a sharp knock with a soft mallet or similar to free it. You should now be able to adjust the stem height with gentle twisting and pulling. If it proves resistant or is stuck, apply WD40 or PlusGas and try again. Coat the hidden part in anti-seize grease and set the stem to the height you want, taking care not to exceed the

maximum height mark. Re-tighten the bolt, then twist the bars from side to side, without undue force, to make sure they are firm.

Headset adjustment

The forks must turn freely, but there must be no trace of play when you rock them back and forth with the front brake on. If adjustment is necessary, some trial and error will be involved.

With a threadless headset slacken the allen bolts securing the stem to the forks one turn. Tighten the allen bolt in the adjusting cap until no play can be felt in the headset. Tighten the stem fixing allen bolts after lining the stem up with the wheel and check that forks still turn smoothly.

With traditional pattern headsets hold the adjustable bearing race in position with a spanner, while loosening the locknut. Reset the adjustable race as appropriate and, keeping it in place, tighten the locknut down onto it. If, no matter how you adjust the headset, you cannot get it right, it will need a complete overhaul, and may need to be replaced.

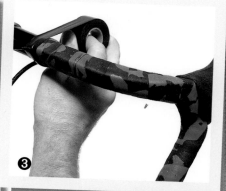

FITTING HANDLEBAR TAPE ❶ Leave about 1cm of overlap at the end of the bars to tuck in later. **❷** A 'figure of eight' may be necessary to avoid bare areas around the levers. **❸** Secure the tape neatly on either side of the bolt.

Crash damage

When you first pick your bike up off the road, the damage may not be very apparent: careful examination may be required to detect it. You should also make these checks when considering buying any second-hand bike.

First, make sure that properly dished and correctly fitted wheels sit centrally in the frame and forks.

A sure sign of something amiss is if the bike has even the slightest tendency not to follow a straight line as you ride it. When it is safe to do so, gingerly lift your hands away from the bars to check this. Carefully inspect around and, in particular, under the top and down tubes, just behind where they meet the head tube, to see if there are bumps or ripples in the tubes. Look down the length of each tube to check that it is straight. The damage here may not be obvious, but is often felt by running a fingertip over the affected area. Wrinkled paint is a sure sign of damage.

The seat and head tubes must be parallel. Stand in front of the bike, slightly to one side, and with one eye closed check the edge of the head tube alongside that of the seat tube behind it. Sighting along a straight edge held beside the head tube will make it easier to judge.

Check that the seat stays are straight by looking at them from directly behind and comparing one with the other. The rear triangle must also be in line with the rest of the frame. Run a piece of fine thread around the rear drop-outs and up around the head tube, then measure the distance between the string and the seat tube on each side; these measurements should be within 3mm of each other.

Sight down the fork blades, checking that they remain parallel and are mirror images of each other all the way down. With the forks facing directly ahead, look at them from the side. Imagine a line going through the

centre of the head tube and then down the centre of the fork blades: are the blades straight, following this line, or are they bent behind it? Lift the wheel and turn the bars from side to side: if the headset binds in one place and feels loose in another, the bike may have a bent fork column or head tube.

Handlebars, stem and brake levers are frequently bent, so examine them from all angles. Check the cranks and pedals by sighting from directly over the bottom bracket: the pedal spindle should remain parallel with the bottom-bracket axle at all points of the revolution. Wheels may have obvious damage, but check the rims for flattened areas, which are often highlighted by a group of loose spokes, and for small dents, especially if your tyre has a pinch puncture. Less obviously, saddle rails and brake callipers can also be bent.

Most modern gear hangers are replaceable, but fixed gear hangers are not, and often get bent. These can be gently realigned with a large adjustable spanner, but it's a tricky process and is best done by a professional mechanic. Faulty realignment can often be the cause of post-crash gear indexing problems.

After any heavy impact you should always check carbon frames and components — especially forks, handlebars and stems. Any sign of cracks and they must be replaced. If they are creaky then strip and reassemble. If creaking persists then replace them — it's not worth risking your life.

Glossary

Terms which have a single reference in the book are explained on the appropriate page. Some common terms, which are used frequently, are listed here for easy reference, plus a selection of obscure terms which you may come across in the racing world.

Anodising   A protective treatment given to aluminium alloy components.

Audax   A non/semi-competitive road event, usually with awards for finishing within a certain time.

Bidon   A French term for a cyclist's feeding bottle.

Bonk   A feeling of total fatigue caused by insufficient calorie intake.

Break/breakaway   A sole rider or group of riders who have ridden ahead of the main bunch in a road race.

Bunch   The main group in a road race. Also called the peloton.

Cadence   The speed of pedal rotation, usually given in revolutions per minute.

Cardiovascular   To do with the heart, lungs and circulatory system.

Cassette   The set of rear cogs.

Chain gang   An informal, but sometimes intense group, training ride.

Cleat   A metal or plastic fitment to the shoe that allows it to lock into the pedal.

Criterium (crit)   A short, fast road race held on a short circuit.

Domestique   A rider whose role is to help and defend the team leader.

Duathlon   A race combining cycling and running.

Echelon   A line of angled riders seeking shelter from a crosswind.

Ergopower   The name given to controls combining the brake and gear operation, made by Campagnolo.

Feed zone   An area designated for helpers to hand up food and drink during a road race.

Free hub   A term originally used by Shimano for a combined rear hub and freewheel mechanism.

Giro   Italian for tour. The Giro d'Italia is the second most important national tour after the Tour de France.

Honk   To ride out of the saddle, standing on the pedals.

Intensity threshold   The highest level of intensity at which an athlete can work without suffering rapid fatigue. Also called the anaerobic threshold.

Jump   See kick.

Kick   An explosive effort made when a sprinter starts an attack or a sprint.

Knock   See bonk.

Line-out   A group of cyclists riding in single file at high speed.

Low-profile (lo-pro)   A time-trial bike with a lowered front end and often a smaller front wheel. A name also given to the bars commonly fitted to lo-pro bikes.

Maglia rosa   The pink jersey awarded to the overall leader in the Giro d'Italia.

Maillot jaune   The yellow jersey awarded to the overall leader in the Tour de France.

Mektronic   A radio controlled electronic rear derailleur made by Mavic.

Modulation   A term used to describe the feeling of braking control.

Monocoque   In cycling, this term is used loosely to mean a bike frame constructed as a single unit, usually from carbon fibre.

Neutral service   Mechanical back-up (e.g. spare wheels) provided by race organisers for all competitors.

Oversize   A term commonly used for larger than usual frame tubing.

Peloton   See bunch.

Prime   A prize awarded at an intermediate point during a road race.

Randonnée   See Audax.

Road bike   A bike used for road racing, rather than simply a bike used on the road (e.g. for time trials, triathlon, touring or training).

Spin   To pedal with a fast, fluid cadence. To spin out is to reach one's maximum cadence.

Sprint   A wheel designed for tubular tyres. (Also a type of track race and a final, rapid effort in any race.)

STI   Shimano Total Integration: combined brake and gear controls made by Shimano.

Toe-clip   A device bolted to the pedals to help secure the feet, now largely replaced by clipless pedal systems with built-in foot-retaining mechanisms.

Triathlon   A race combining cycling, running and swimming.

Tubular tyre (tub)   A very light and supple racing tyre with the inner tube sewn inside the tyre casing.

UCI (Union Cycliste Internationale)   The international governing body for competitive cycling.

Addresses

Cycle racing is an organised sport dependent on national and international bodies. Membership or affiliation through a local club is usually essential to race, and generally includes insurance. Clubs are normally your entry point into competitive cycling and provide encouragement, technical and training advice, and, not least, comradeship. The national organisations listed should be able to provide details of local clubs and those catering for specialist interests.

BELGIUM
K. Belgische Wielrijdersbond
Royal Ligue Vélocipédique Belge
Avenue du Globe 49
1190 Bruxelles
Tel: (+ 32) (0)2 349 1911/2
Web site: www.kbwb-rlvb.be

CANADA
Canadian Cycling Association
2197 Riverside Drive, Suite 203
Ottawa
Ontario K1H7X3
Tel (+ 1) 613 2481353
www.canadian-cycling.com

CZECH REPUBLIC
Czech Cycling Federation
Nad Hhlinikem 4/1186
150 00 Praha 5
Tel: (+ 420) (2) 52 61 29/57 21 03 72
www.csc-cystlik.a.cz

DENMARK
Danmarks Cykle Union
Idrættens Hus
DK-2605 Brøndby
Tel: (+ 45) 43 262 202
E-mail: dcu@dcu.cykllng.dk

FINLAND
Suomen Pyöräivyunioni
Radiokatu 20
00240 Helsinki
Tel: (+ 358) 9 278 6575
E-mail: spu@kolumbus.fl
www.pyoraily.fi

FRANCE
Fédération Française de Cyclisme
ZAC de Nanteuil
Bâtiment Jean Monnet
5 Rue de Rome
93561 Rosny-Sous-Bois (Cedex)
Tel: (+ 33) (0)1 49 356 900
Web site: www.ffc.fr
(Racing)

Fédération Française de Cyclotourisme
8 Rue Jean-Marie Jégo
75013 Paris
Tel: (+ 33) (0)144 168 888
Web site: www.ffct.fr
(Cycle-touring)

GERMANY
Bund Deutscher Radfahrer
Otto-Fleck-Schneisse 4
6528 Frankfurt/Main
Tel: (+ 49) (0)69 967 8000
E-mail: info@bdr-online.org
www.rad.net.de

ITALY
Federazione Ciclistica Italiana
Studio Olimpico – Curva Nord
Cancello L – Porta 91
00194 Roma
Tel: (+ 39) (0)6 368 57813/57255
Fax: (+ 39) (0)6 368 57175
www.fererciclismo.it

IRELAND
Federation of Irish Cyclists
Kelly Roche House
619 North Circular Road
Dublin 1
Tel: (+ 353) (0)1 855 1522
Fax: (+ 353) (0)1 855 1771
www.cyclingireland.ie
(All forms of competitive cycling and structured leisure cycling)

NETHERLANDS
Koninklijke Nederlansche Wielren Unie
Postbus 2661
3430 GB Nieuwegein
Tel (+ 31) (0)307 513300
www.knwu.ni

POLAND
Union Cycliste de Pologne
1 Rue Andrezeja
05-800 Pruszkun
Tel (+ 48) 22 7288534
www.pzkol.pl

SPAIN
Federación Española Ciclismo
Ferraz 16-5
E-28008 Madrid
Tel: (+ 34) 91 542 0421/542 2139

SWEDEN
Svenska Cykelförbundet
Idtrettenshuss
Fiskartorpsvagen 15A
S-11473
Stockholm 468
Tel (+ 69) 9630066
www.scf.se

UNITED KINGDOM
British cycle sport is very fragmented:
a number of organisations cover
various interests.

British Cycling
National Cycling Centre
1 Stuart Street
Manchester M11 4DQ
Tel: (+ 44) (0)870 871 2000
www.britishcycling.org.uk
*(Administers competitive cycling, except
time trials. There are affiliated
federations for Scotland, Wales and
Northern Ireland.)*

Road Time Trials Council
77 Arlington Drive
Pennington,
Leigh WN7 3QP
Tel: (+ 44) (0)1942 603 976
Web site: www.rttc.org.uk

*(Administers time-trial events in England
and Wales)*

Cyclists' Touring Club
69 Meadrow
Godalming
Surrey GU7 3HS
Tel: (+ 44) (0)1483 417 217
Web site: www.ctc.org.uk
*(Primarily a touring and campaign
organsisation)*

AUSTRALIA
Cycling Australia
PO Box 7183
Bass Hill
NSW 2197
Tel (+ 61) (02)9644 3002
www.cycling.org.au

UNITED STATES
USA Cycling Inc
One Olympic Plaza
Colorado Springs
80909 - 577
Tel: (+ 1) 719 578 4581
Web site: www.usacycling.org

INTERNATIONAL
Union Cycliste Internationale
(UCI)
37 Route de Chavannes
CH 1007 Lausanne
Switzerland
Tel: (+ 41) (0)21 622 05 80
Web site: www.uci.ch
*(The international governing body for
cycle sport)*

Index

ACKNOWLEDGEMENTS

The publishers would like to thank the following manufacturers and suppliers for kindly providing props for photography:

Argos Racing Cycles: frame tubes, brazed joint; **Bell Helmets; Blue Ridge**: Look pedal system, adjustable stem; **BMC; Campagnolo SRL**: Campagnolo Record 10-speed groupset; **Dave Bater Cycles, Bristol**: Bianchi bike with threadless headset, Profile integrated handlebars; **DT Swiss; Fisher Outdoor Leisure; Giant Bicycles; Geoffrey Butler Cycles**: track bike; **Giro Helmets; Ison Distribution**: various tools; **Madison Cycles Plc**: Park tools and workstand, water bottles and cages; **Mavic**: wheels, rims; **Raleigh Industries Ltd**: Raleigh bikes, parts and accessories; **RJ Chicken & Sons Ltd**: Time pedal system, TA chainsets; **Royce UK Ltd**: titanium bottom-bracket cartridge; **St John Street Cycles**: Cannondale bike; **SBC (UK) Ltd**: Specialized wheel, track mitts; **Scott UK**: Scott triathlon bike; **Sonic Cycles**: Primax headset; **Trek USA**: Trek bike; **Velo Direct**: HED wheel.

The publishers would also like to thank: Select Cycle Components; Michael Elson; Karrimor (John North) and Mark Creaby for modelling the position photos.

Ben Searle would like to thank the following: Mike Burrows and Greg Fuquay for specialised technical information, Russell Gasser for some late-night techno-babble discussion and Hilary Stone for running an eye over the general technical content and for loan of props.
Steve Thomas would like to thank Clive Powell and Martin Earley for their help and assistance.